"My Name Was Martha"

"My Name Was Martha"

A Renaissance Woman's
Autobiographical Poem

by
Martha Moulsworth

Edited with Commentary by
Robert C. Evans and Barbara Wiedemann

LOCUST HILL PRESS
West Cornwall, CT
1993

Library of Congress Cataloging-in-Publication Data

Moulsworth, Martha.
  My name was Martha : a Renaissance woman's autobiographical
poem / by Martha Moulsworth : edited with commentary by
Robert C. Evans and Barbara Wiedemann.
    117p.   cm.
    ISBN 0-933951-53-1 : $22.50
    1. Women--England--History--Renaissance, 1450-1600-
-Poetry. 2. Women--England--History--17th century--Poetry.
3. Women--England--Biography--Poetry.   I. Evans, Robert C.
II. Wiedemann, Barbara.   III. Title.
PR2323.M67M9 1993
821'.4--dc20   93-27167
                                                                    CIP

Printed on acid-free, 250-year-life paper
Manufactured in the United States of America

in memory of
EMMA SCHALL EVANS
(1917–1992)
loving and beloved

"All measure,
and all language,
we should pass,
Should we tell
what a miracle
she was."

CONTENTS

Acknowledgments • *ix*

Preface • *xi*

Chapter 1: The Poem Itself: Text and Analysis • *3*
    The Memorandum of Martha Moulsworth • *4*
    Textual Notes • *9*
    The Poem as Work of Art • *13*

Chapter 2: Historical Contexts • *39*
    I. Women and Education • *40*
    II. Women as Daughters • *44*
    III. Women as Wives • *49*
    IV. Women as Widows • *57*

Chapter 3: The Poem as Autobiography • *71*

Chapter 4: Feminist Contexts • *93*

Bibliography • *109*

ACKNOWLEDGMENTS

Jim Barfoot has been a special friend to this project and to us both, and we wish to thank him for his constant encouragement.

We also owe special thanks to the very helpful staff of the Beinecke Rare Book and Manuscript Library at Yale University. In particular we wish to thank William Larsh for his assistance, and especially Stephen Parks, Curator of the Osborn Collection, for granting permission to reproduce the text of Martha Moulsworth's "Memorandum." Our first acquaintance with Moulsworth could not have occurred in a more hospitable place than the Beinecke.

Our work on this project has both introduced us to and reminded us of some of the extraordinarily valuable work that has been accomplished over the past two decades on the topic of women in literature, history, and critical theory. Our text and notes attempt to acknowledge more fully our debts to such work, and we hope that this book will help call further attention not only to a valuable piece of writing by a particular woman, but also to the stimulating work that has been done on women's writing in general.

Grants from the National Endowment for the Humanities, the Folger Shakespeare Library, and the Research Grant-in-Aid program at Auburn University at Montgomery aided our work at various stages, and we wish to thank those institutions and their staffs.

As this project unfolded, various students in various classes shared their insightful responses to Moulsworth's poem. We especially want to thank the students enrolled in the Fall 1992 class on early seventeenth century literature and those in the Spring 1993 course dealing with literary criticism. Their lively, thoughtful reactions made them teachers as well as students.

Certain students in particular have contributed, in one way or another, to the encouraging mental climate in which this project was nurtured. Kurt Niland, more a colleague than a student, helped check the manuscript; he, Forrest, and Amy (she of the powder-blue dress) were present from the start. Thanks are also due to Julliana Ooi and Philip Ding (armed with gun and seaweed); to Phil Festoso (visitor from France); to Joseph T. Roy, Jr. ("Tireless" is his middle name); to Lynn Bryan (the laughing Latinist); and to Mike Crocker (man of few words but big heart).

Friends and colleagues who deserve special thanks include David Brumble, Anne Little, Jan Dudle, David Walker, David Witkosky, Eduardo Gargurevich, Julie Novak, and, of course, Linda Stringer, the dynamic doyenne.

This project could not have had a better shepherd than Tom Bechtle.

Finally, we wish to thank some special women who, in their strength of character, remind us very much of Martha Moulsworth. These include Nichole, Carol, Claramae, Darla, Betty, the incomparable Ruth, and the small, strong, sustaining woman to whom this book is dedicated.

August 3, 1993

PREFACE

The past two decades have witnessed a growing interest in the experiences and writings of early modern women. Historians and literary scholars have cooperated to exhume, examine, and often extol the neglected lives and works of women who lived during a period when the idea of a female writer could seem almost an oxymoron. Thousands of documents have been quarried and hundreds of texts have been edited and critically assessed, so that today we have not only a richer body of historical evidence but also a richer canon of literary works. However, one text that seems to have been overlooked is a long, previously unpublished autobiographical poem that should prove equally interesting to social historians and literary critics. Entitled "The Memorandum of Martha Moulsworth / Widdowe," the poem is fascinating for a number of reasons.[1]

In the first place, Moulsworth's "Memorandum" is a poem that both merits and rewards close reading; it is not a meandering autobiographical hodge-podge but a work that displays considerable skill, artistry, and thematic coherence. It would be an interesting poem whether or not its author were a woman; the fact that it *was* written by a female only makes it all the more intriguing. Secondly, the poem's date of composition can be precisely pin-pointed, and the period of time it covers—fifty-five years, from 1577 to 1632—is not only intriguingly vast, but also encompasses some of the most important decades of English history. In addition, the poem expresses opinions, particularly about women's access to universities and the ideal purposes of schooling, that would seem to make Moulsworth one of the earliest English advocates of truly equal education. At the same time, however, Moulsworth's poem also suggests a highly complex attitude toward her status in a rigidly patriarchal society, including her

xi

relations with her God, her father, and her three successive husbands. The poem offers a complicated mixture of self-assertion and deference, of shrewdness and wisdom, of self-respect and selfless love. Yet these are only a few causes of its significance. Moulsworth's poem is intriguing first and foremost in its own right, as a work of art. But its interest seems all the more obvious when it is seen in light of various historical, literary, and theoretical contexts.

This book, then, has several complementary purposes. Its chief aim is to provide an accurate transcription of Moulsworth's text as it appears in the original manuscript. We have resisted the temptation to modernize spelling or "clarify" punctuation, especially since some of the apparent ambiguities of Moulsworth's punctuation seem ambiguous in meaningful ways. To have imposed punctuation on certain lines or phrases would have meant restricting their range of meaning or significance. In any case, Moulsworth's poem makes more than enough sense as it presently stands; for that reason, tinkering with its punctuation seems all the more pointless. Nevertheless, explanatory notes have been appended to the poem in order to clarify some of Moulsworth's allusions, to comment on some of her word choices, to discuss ambiguities in the manuscript, and to provide other useful information.

The discussion of the poem that concludes the first chapter is intentionally full and detailed. Moulsworth seems to have written her work with deliberate and self-conscious skill, and the analysis provided in our first chapter attempts to offer a patient and attentive reading of the poem *as* a poem. We hope that this interpretation can begin to do some justice to the poem's subtle artistry and rich implications. This "close reading" may seem deliberately old-fashioned and "formalist," because it is. Rather than treating the poem first and foremost as a biographical, historical, sociological, political, or discursive document, the first chapter attempts to treat it as a highly complex work of art. By doing so, that chapter hopes to pay Moulsworth the compliment of treating her not simply as a woman writer, or as a woman who happened to write, but as a skillful writer who happened to be a woman. No one can deny that her sex and gender were important, and in fact Moulsworth herself repeatedly stresses how both factors shaped her life and her poem. The emphasis of our first chapter, however, is primarily on the poem's artistry as such.[2]

Subsequent chapters try to supplement this account by attempting to place the poem in various contexts and by trying to approach it from various perspectives. Chapter 2, for instance, tries to look at the work in light of its historical contexts, especially in light of the various roles and experiences of Renaissance women. In particular, this chapter focuses on women's roles as daughters, wives, and widows, and it also looks at the status and limits of women's education during the early modern period. Chapter 3 attempts to view the poem specifically as a piece of *autobiographical* writing, since Moulsworth's work seems important as one of the earliest examples of such writing by anyone in England, male or female. Finally, Chapter 4 tries to view the poem in light of recent feminist theories about the nature and features of writing by women.

We hope that this book will prove useful, then, not only as an edition and discussion of a significant but previously unpublished poem, but also as an overview of some important issues in historiography, autobiography, and feminist theory. Our chief goal is to make the poem available in a useful format. Our second goal is to try to begin to understand the poem as a work of art. Our related goals are to try to place Moulsworth and her writing in contexts that will illuminate not only them, but also the experiences and writings of other early modern women.

Robert Evans wrote the first three chapters; Barbara Wiedemann provided Chapter 4. Any faults in the first three chapters are therefore the responsibility of Barbara Wiedemann, who is also responsible for any shortcomings in Chapter 4. This Preface was written by Robert Evans.

Notes

1. Betty Travitsky notes that Renaissance English women usually made little effort to publicize or even print their own literary efforts, and certainly Moulsworth's poem seems to fit this pattern. See *The Paradise of Women: Writings by Englishwomen of the Renaissance* (New York: Columbia University Press, 1989),

114. Sara Heller Mendelson notes the scarcity of sources offering a direct record of women's everyday experiences during the Stuart period, a fact that only enhances the value of Moulsworth's poem. See her essay "Stuart Women's Diaries and Occasional Memoirs," in *Women in English Society 1500–1800*, ed. Mary Prior (London and New York: Methuen, 1985), 181–210, esp. 181.

2. By exploring the *poetic* achievement of Moulsworth's poem, rather than treating it simply as an historical document, we seek to show it the same consideration one might show to a similar work produced by an early modern male. In so doing, we seek to avoid a pitfall noted by Marlene Kadar, who observes that a highly political approach to women's writing often causes us to "patronize when what we want to do is include." See her essay "Coming to Terms: Life Writing—from Genre to Critical Practice," in *Essays on Life Writing: From Genre to Critical Practice*, ed. Marlene Kadar (Toronto: University of Toronto Press, 1992), 3–20; for the quoted passage, see 8. In this respect we are also in sympathy with Shirley Neuman's call for a "poetics of differences," which she defines as "a praxis that would emphasize the *textual particularities* of autobiographies and would foreground the knowledge borne by *their* narrators' saying 'I' rather than subsume those particularities, that knowledge, under categories that are often *in*different to them." See her essay "Autobiography: From Different Poetics to a Poetics of Differences," in *Essays on Life Writing: From Genre to Critical Practice*, ed. Marlene Kadar, 213–30; for the quoted passage, see 225–26.

"My Name Was Martha"

Chapter 1

THE POEM ITSELF:
TEXT AND ANALYSIS

The manuscript of Martha Moulsworth's "Memorandum" occurs in a commonplace book (Osborn MS fb 150) currently housed in the Beinecke Library at Yale University. Although the pages on which the poem appears are unnumbered, the work occurs near the end of the manuscript volume. The poem is preceded by many blank pages, although most of the other texts included in this commonplace book are political in nature. Moulsworth's poem is written in a neat, relatively clear hand from the early seventeenth century. Whether the handwriting is her own is uncertain. In the following transcription, line numbers have been added in square brackets. Brackets have also been used to set off the various marginal notes that run alongside the manuscript version of the poem itself; these notes were apparently composed by Moulsworth. In the transcript, punctuation and spelling have been left unchanged, and in the few places where a word is missing, crossed out, or corrected, these facts have been appropriately indicated.

The symbol (†) preceding a line indicates the presence of a note pertaining to that line in the *"Textual Notes"* section, pp. 9–12.

Nouember the 10th 1632
†   The Memorandum of Martha Moulsworth
Widdowe

The tenth day of the winter month Nouember
A day which I must duely still remember
did open first theis eis, and shewed this light
† Now on thatt day* vppon thatt daie I write

Nouember 10th 1632

This season fitly willinglie combines   [5
the birth day of my selfe, & of theis lynes
† The tyme the clocke, the yearly stroke is one
thatt clocke by ffiftie fiue retourns hath gonn
How ffew, how many warnings itt will giue
he only knowes in whome we are, & liue   [10

[*beginning next to line 7:* my muse is a tell
clocke, & echoeth[?]
euerie stroke wth
a coupled ryme
so many tymes
viz 55
Acts 17 28 &[?]

In carnall state of sin originall
I did nott stay one whole day naturall
The seale of grace in Sacramentall water
so soone had I, so soone become the daughter
of earthly parents, & of heauenlie ffather   [15
† some christen late for state, the wiser rather.

† My Name was Martha, Martha tooke much payne

[Luke 10: 14

our Sauiour christ her guesse [*sic*] to entertayne
God gyue me grace my Inward house to dight
that he wth me may supp, & stay all night   [20

[Reuel: 3.20:

My ffather was a Man of spottles ffame

[Luke 24.29

of gentle Birth, & Dorsett was his name
He had, & left lands of his owne possession
he was of Leuies tribe by his profession
his Mother oxford knowenge well his worth   [25
arayd in scarlett Robe did send him fforth.
By him I was brought vpp in godlie pietie
In modest chearefullnes, & sad sobrietie
Nor onlie so, Beyond my sex & kind
he did wth learning Lattin decke mind [*sic*]   [30
And whie nott so? the muses ffemalls are
and therfore of Vs ffemales take some care
Two Vniuersities we haue of men
o thatt we had but one of women then

———

O then thatt would in witt, and tongs surpasse   [35
All art of men thatt is, or euer was
But I of Lattin haue no cause to boast
ffor want of vse, I longe agoe itt lost

[Lattin is not the most
marketable mariadge
mettall

Had I no other portion to my dowre
I might have stood a virgin to this houre   [40
Butt though the virgin Muses I loue well
I haue longe since Bid virgin life ffarewell

Thrice this Right hand did holly wedlocke plight

† And thrice this Left with pledged ringe was dight

  three husbands me, & I haue them enioyde   [45

  Nor I by them, nor they by me annoyde

  all louely, lovinge all, some more, some lesse

  though gonn their loue, & memorie I blesse.

  Vntill my one & twentieth yeare of Age

                           [1 Husband, Mr Nicolas

                           Prynne, Aprill 18

                           1598

  I did nott bind my selfe in Mariadge   [50

  My springe was late, some thinke thatt sooner loue

† butt backward springs doe oft the kindest proue

  My first knott held fiue yeares, & eight months more

† then was a yeare sett on my mourninge score

  My second bond tenn years nine months did last   [55

                         [2^d Mr Tho: Througood

                         ffebruary 3 1604

† three years eight Months I kept a widowes ffast

  The third I tooke a louely man, & kind

† such comlines in age we seldome ffind

                         [3^d Mr Beuill

                         Moulswoorth

                         June 15, 1619

† ffrom Mortimers he drewe his pedigre

† their Arms he ~~bought~~ bore, not bought wth Heraulds fee   [60

  third wife I was to him, as he to me

  third husband was, in nomber we agree

  eleuen years, & eight months his autume lasted

  a second spring to soone awaie it hasted

was neuer man so Buxome to his wife [65
wth him I led an easie darlings life.
I had my will in house, in purse in Store
what would a women old or yong haue more?

Two years Almost outwearinge since he died
And yett, & yett my tears ffor him nott dried [70
I by the ffirst, & last some Issue had
butt roote, & ffruite is dead, wch makes me sad

———

My husbands all on holly dayes did die
Such day, such waie, they to the S^{ts} did hye
This life is worke-day euen att the Best [75
butt christian death, an holly day of Rest
the ffirst, the ffirst of Martirs did befall
St Stevens ffeast to him was ffunerall
the morrowe after christ our fflesh did take
this husband did his mortall fflesh fforsake [80
the second on a double sainted day
to Jude, & Symon tooke his happy way
This Symon as an auncient Story Sayth
did ffirst in England plant the Christian ffayth
                                        [Niceph: Histo:
Most sure itt is that Jude in holy writt [85
                                [Jude ver: 3
doth warne vs to Mayntayne, & ffight ffor itt
In wch all those that liue, & die, may well
hope wth the S^{ts} eternally to dwell
The last on St Mathias day did wend
vnto his home, & pilgrimages ende [90
this feast comes in that season wch doth bringe
vppon dead Winters cold, a lyvelie Springe

His Bodie winteringe in the lodge of death
Shall ffeele A springe, wth budd of life, & Breath
† And Rise in incorruption, glorie, power   [95
                                                            [corrin: 15.42
† Like to the Bodie of our Sauiour
                                                            [phillip: 3.21

In vayne itt were, prophane itt were ffor me
† W^th Sadnes to aske wch of theis three
                                                            [Matt: 22.18

I shall call husband in ye Resurrection
ffor then shall all in glorious perfection   [100
Like to th'immortall heauenlie Angells liue
who wedlocks bonds doe neither take nor giue
                                                            [verse 30

But in the Meane tyme this must be my care
of knittinge here a fourth knott to beware
† A threefold cord though hardlie yett is broken   [105
Another Auncient storie doth betoken
                                                            [Ecclesiast 4.12

† thatt seldome comes A Better; whie should I
then putt my Widowehood in jeopardy?
the Virgins life is gold, as Clarks vs tell
the Widowes siluar, I loue siluar well.   [110

###

Textual Notes

Title: "Memorandum": literally, "[It is] to be remembered"; with perhaps the additional sense of a memento or souvenir of Moulsworth's life.

4: "on thatt day* vppon that day": probably wordplay meaning "on that same day and also about or concerning that day"

7: In Moulsworth's marginal note, the spelling and meaning of the word followed by a boldface question mark are not entirely certain. This is one of the few cases in the MS where the handwriting has proven difficult to decipher. Clearly the word is a verb, and "echoeth" best fits the handwriting and makes the most sense in context. "Tell clocke": according to the OED, one who "tells the clock," meaning "to count the hours as shown by a clock; hence, to pass one's time idly." The final part of the Biblical citation is also unclear and thus concludes with an added question mark in boldface. Probably the phrasing intended was "&c" (i.e., "etc."). That is, Moulsworth clearly alludes to Acts 17: 28, but she may also find the following few verses relevant to her meaning: "For in him we live, and move, and have our being; as certain also of your own poets have said, For we are also his offspring.... he hath appointed a day, in which he will judge the world in righteousness by *that* man whom he hath ordained" (Acts 17: 28–31). Interestingly, one of those who responded to Paul's call in this instance was "a woman named Damaris" (Acts 17: 34).

16: "for state": with a view toward public dignity, pomp, and ceremony; "rather": earlier

17: Moulsworth seems to have misremembered or miscopied the location of the reference to Martha, which should be Luke 10: 41. In context the passage reads as follows: "Now it came to pass, as they went, that he entered into a certain village; and a certain woman, named Martha, received him into her house. And she had a sister, called Mary, who also sat at Jesus' feet, and heard his word. But Martha was cumbered about much serving, and came to him, and said, Lord, dost thou not care that my sister hath left me to serve alone? Bid her, therefore, that she help me. And Jesus answered, and said unto her, Martha, Martha, thou

art careful and troubled about many things. But one thing is need-
ful, and Mary hath chosen that good part, which shall not be
taken away from her" (Luke 10: 38–42). St. Martha was tradi-
tionally considered the "prototype of the busy housewife." See
J.C.J. Metford, *Dictionary of Christian Lore and Legend* (New
York: Thames and Hudson, 1983), 168.

18: "guesse": guest.

20: "Behold, I stand at the door, and knock; if any man hear my
voice, and open the door, I will come in to him, and will sup with
him, and he with me" (Revelation 3: 20). The next scriptural ci-
tation also seems relevant to this line: "But they constrained
him, saying, Abide with us; for it is toward evening, and the day
is far spent. And he went in to tarry with them" (Luke 24: 29).

24: "Leuies tribe": among the ancient Hebrews, the Levites were a
religious caste descended from Levi, son of Jacob. They held no
portion of land in Canaan (Deuteronomy 18). Perhaps this fact is
relevant to Moulsworth's claim in l. 23 about her father's lands.
Presumably he was a clergyman of some sort.

26: Scarlet colored robes were traditionally presented to doctors
of divinity or the law.

28: "sad": settled, firmly established; strong; orderly, grave, se-
rious; dignified; mature (*OED*).

30: Surely this was meant to read "decke my mind."

38: "want of vse": lack of practice or exercise.

44: "dight": adorned, prepared.

52: "backward": late, delayed.

54: "score": record or account; the sum recorded to a customer's
debit (*OED*).

56: "widowes ffast": abstinence as an expression of grief.

58: Moulsworth is mentioned in a letter dated 1603, written by Sir
Robert Cecil (chief minister of James I) and addressed to the Lord
Chief Baron and the other Barons of the Exchequer: "I am certi-
fied by my deputies in my farm of silk that Henry Southworth
and Bevill Mowlsworth, two of his Majesty's waiters of the port
of London, have been much envied by some of the officers of the
port, and often unjustly molested by others both for their endeav-
ours to serve his Majesty and their diligence to assist my

deputies.... I understand also that an English bill is depending before you in the Court of Exchequer preferred by one William Gerrard against Moulsworth and Southworth, which I am informed is but matter of molestation, because the suit is not brought against them by due form of law.... As I am not willing to entreat for any favour if they have evil demeaned themselves, so am I unwilling they should endure unjust molestation for their employment in my farm, or be hindered from his Majesty's service.... I knowing well what is fit to be recommended to persons in your place, who are to proceed upon proofs and not allegations, do only in general show you my desire to have them favoured as far as is reasonable." Well before he married Martha, then, Moulsworth seems to have been a man who enjoyed some influence and connections. See Great Britain, Historical Manuscripts Commission, *Calendar of the Manuscripts of the ... Marquess of Salisbury*, part XV (London: HMSO, 1930), 362–63.

59: "Mortimers": an ancient noble family, especially prominent in the fourteenth century.

60: "Heraulds fee": this alludes to the notorious abuses by which bogus coats of arms could be purchased from corrupt heralds. The cancelled word appears this way in the manuscript.

65: "Buxome": Gracious, indulgent, favorable; obliging, amiable, courteous, affable, kindly; blithe, jolly; obedient, compliant, humble (*OED*).

67: "Store": provision and maintenance of household necessities.

72: "roote, & ffruite": this pairing of words has Biblical precedents; see, for instance, Proverbs 12: 12.

75: "worke-day": probably a variant of "work-a-day"—i.e., routine, laborious; distinguished from a holiday or day of rest.

77–78: For details of St. Stephen, see Acts 6–7, esp. 7: 54–60. His holiday falls on 26 December.

81–82: 28 October. "Apart from appearing in lists of the Apostles and being present at Pentecost, Simon receives scant attention in the [New Testament], but legend links his later exploits with those of St. Jude. According to Craton's *Ten Books* (probably dating from the 4th century) and Abdias's *Apostolic History* (617–21), the two apostles conducted their evangelical missions in Syria, Mesopotamia and Persia" (Metford 228).

83: Thomas Fuller, in his *Church History of Great Britain* (ed. J. S. Brewer, 6 vols. [Oxford: Oxford University Press, 1845]) cites as the source of this legend Dorotheus, whom he identifies as the "bishop of Tyre under Diocletian and Constantine the Great" (1: 11–12).

84: The marginal note probably refers to Nicephorus Callistus (ca. 1256–ca. 1335), a Byzantine historian, whose "principal work, a 'Church History,' narrates in 18 books the events from the birth of Christ to the death of the Phocas (610).... In 1555 it was translated into Latin and played an important part in the controversial literature of the time.... " See *The Oxford Dictionary of the Christian Church*, ed. F.L. Cross (London: Oxford University Press, 1966), 953.

86: "... ye should earnestly contend for the faith which was once delivered unto the saints" (Jude, verse 3).

89: Saint Matthias's day is 24 February.

95: 1 Corinthians 15: 42 says of "the resurrection of the dead" that "It is sown in corruption; it is raised in incorruption."

96: Philippians 3: 21 promises that Christ "shall change our vile body, that it may be fashioned like his glorious body, according to the working by which he is able even to subdue all things unto himself."

98: The Sadducees, "who say that there is no resurrection," confronted Jesus with the story of a woman who had been married successively to seven brothers, all of whom died. They continued: "Therefore, in the resurrection whose wife shall she be of the seven? For they all had her. Jesus answered and said unto them, Ye do err, not knowing the scriptures, nor the power of God. For in the resurrection they neither marry, nor are given in marriage, but are like the angels of God in heaven" (Matthew 21: 23, 28–30).

105: "a threefold cord is not quickly broken" (Ecclesiastes 4: 12).

107: For the proverb "seldom comes the better," which was widely current in the sixteenth century, see Morris Palmer Tilley, *A Dictionary of the Proverbs in England in the Sixteenth and Seventeenth Centuries* (Ann Arbor: University of Michigan Press, 1950), 46.

THE POEM AS WORK OF ART

The importance of Martha Moulsworth's "Memorandum" as an historical document should be obvious: as one of the few early modern texts in which a woman speaks for and of herself, the poem would be of interest even if it possessed little poetic merit.[1] Fortunately, however, Moulsworth's poem possesses considerable value in its own right, as a work of art—as a thoughtful demonstration of linguistic skill, thematic coherence, and structural design. Moulsworth seems to have wanted to do more than set down the main events of her life; she obviously wanted to impose on those events (or to find in them) a significant shape and meaning.[2] The mere fact that the poem is so obviously patterned in its larger structure—with fifty-five couplets to complement Moulsworth's fifty-five years—invites attention to other patterns of meaning, other indications of design. As it happens, such design and patterns abound; Moulsworth was obviously a highly self-conscious, conscientious writer who sought quite deliberately to exploit many of the rhetorical resources of her language.[3] Her poem's texture is thick with assonance, alliteration, word-play, meaningful ambiguities, and other devices of sound and meaning. It reveals a fondness both for balanced syntactical units and for sudden, ironic juxtapositions. Indeed, sustaining and recovering balance are two of the poem's most important implicit themes; the work displays both artistic and emotional equilibrium.[4] In fact, the first sort of balance helps reinforce and convey the second; the maturity and wisdom of Moulsworth's tone and attitude are at once reflected and created through the careful craft with which her poem is put together. Moulsworth plays with words, but she rarely does so in ways that seem simply self-indulgent. In her poem as in all accomplished works, artistic skill both registers and reinforces meaning. Only a close reading of the "Memorandum" can begin to do justice to its aesthetic complexity.

Time—its passage, pains, joys, and redemption—is one of the most obvious organizing themes of Moulsworth's poem. She calls attention to this theme through repeated references to days, months, years, and seasons, and she continually alludes to Biblical and secular history to provide a larger perspective on her own

experience.[5] Certainly the theme of time is powerfully empha-
sized in the poem's opening line, a line typical of Moulsworth's
larger work in both its subject and its style. The poem's very first
words stress a specific date, a specific moment in the present in a
work later preoccupied with the past and future. Characteristi-
cally, Moulsworth accentuates the importance of this particular
moment through balanced syntax, using one adjective-noun phrase
("tenth day") to balance and reinforce another ("winter month";
l. 1). Pairing the phrases gives each a force it would separately
lack, and, as will be seen, this kind of syntactical equilibrium is
utterly typical of Moulsworth's style throughout the poem. The
tactic appears again, for instance, not only in the repetition of
"day" in l. 2, but also in l. 3, where Moulsworth explains how this
date did not only "open first theis eis," but also "shewed this
light." Just as the birthday of the author coincides with the cre-
ation of the poem, so the beginning of mental perception coincides
with the moment of physical revelation. In a poem so much con-
cerned with death, Moulsworth begins by emphasizing literal
and figurative life—the birth of the body as well as the awaken-
ing of the senses and consciousness. Yet this emphasis on new be-
ginnings is also framed by the opening reference to "winter"—the
first of many references to the seasons, but also a reference that
reinforces the poem's stress on endings, on the conclusions of natu-
ral cycles. The birth of both Moulsworth and her poem in "the
winter month Nouember" is at once literally true and richly sym-
bolic; her life began in the midst of a season associated with
death, and the poem that sums up that life takes shape in both a
literal and a figurative winter.

Balanced pairings continue to be important features of the
poem's first few lines. Such pairings not only emphasize the sense
of equilibrium so important to the poem's larger mood, but they
also highlight the distinctive importance of each pair's ele-
ments. Pairing the words invites us to notice their differences as
well as their similarities, so that each word achieves maximum
impact. This is true of such pairings as "fitly willinglie" in l. 5,
"my selfe" and "theis lynes" in l. 6, "clocke" and "stroke" in l. 7,
"ffew" and "many" in l. 9, and especially "are" and "liue" in l. 10.
That last pairing stresses God's role as both creator and sus-
tainer—the Being Who permits our being and Who also under-
girds our continued existence. It hardly seems an accident that

Moulsworth's first reference to God occurs in l. 10, since ten was a number traditionally associated with perfection and order.[6] Numerological patterning is obviously important to this poem, in which fifty-five couplets parallel the author's fifty-five years. Thus it seems highly appropriate that Moulsworth's first reference to God, and her particular emphasis on his powers of creation and sustenance, should occur in a line numerically suited to both subjects.

Such numerical patterning is only one of many ways in which Moulsworth seeks to impose an order on the story of her life—or rather, to discern the shapes and orders her life implies. The balanced structure of the poem contributes to its mood of calm equilibrium, and certainly another of the work's prominent features also suggests this notion of a life lived within a larger scheme of significance. This feature involves the poem's many explicit Biblical allusions. In using these, Moulsworth is hardly subtle; in fact, she does everything possible to call attention to them, not only echoing specific Biblical phrasing but also providing precise marginal citations of book, chapter, and verse. The first of these, in l. 10, aptly coincides with the first explicit reference to God; the allusion to Acts 17: 28 reminds us that "in him we live, and move, and have our being." By invoking the Bible so insistently and repeatedly, Moulsworth reinforces an idea she has already strongly implied—that as she is the author of her poem, so God is the author of her life. Just as she fashions a text from her existence, so the full meaning of her existence is continually illuminated by the text (the Bible) already fashioned by God. Moulsworth proves herself an intent and diligent reader of the scriptures, but her poem also suggests the ways in which the scriptures have already read—or made sense of—her life. Part of the calm, calming effect of Moulsworth's poem derives precisely from this sense that she does not need so much to impose an order on her biography as to discover and elucidate the order it already implies.[7]

Typical of Moulsworth's use of balanced juxtapositions is the shift that occurs between lines 10 and 11. No sooner does she remind us that she is one of God's "offspring" (Acts 17: 29) than she immediately also reminds us that she was scarred from birth by "sin originall" (l. 11). Typically, the line emphasizing her fallen condition is itself balanced, with the adjective-noun phrase "carnall state" paired off against the noun-adjective phrase "sin originall." Typically, too, Moulsworth immediately balances the reference to original sin with a reference to holy baptism; it was thanks to baptism that she "did nott stay one whole day naturall" but achieved the "seale of grace in Sacramentall water" (ll. 12–13). The quick shift from the emphasis on sin to the even more emphatic stress on redemption parallels the quickness with which Moulsworth's parents acted to have her baptized, and this speed is itself stressed through the balanced repetition of "soone" in l. 14. By the same token, such balance is stressed again in l. 15, in which she refers to herself as the daughter "of earthly parents, & of heauenlie ffather." Similarly careful phrasing is evident in the next line, in which "state" echoes "late" to reinforce, perhaps, the concern with external display that Moulsworth implicitly criticizes (l. 16). Here as elsewhere in the poem, she distinguishes her own experiences and the motives that shaped them from those of others, but she does so in an understated way that exemplifies self-content rather than contempt or pride.

In this as in so many ways, her poem displays the balance it extols. Such balance, for instance, is also exhibited by the way this six-line section of the poem closes. Line 16 juxtaposes the notions of "late" with early ("rather") christening, but by explicitly emphasizing christening, the line also implicitly balances the stress in l. 11 on the "carnall state of sin originall." Moreover, line 16 suggests both a concern with death and an answer to it, and death, of course, will soon prove one of the poem's most prominent themes. Here that theme is merely implied; later it is much more obviously emphasized. For the moment, however, Moulsworth is cunningly subtle in the ways she broaches the notion. Typical, for example, is the understated but nonetheless somewhat startling use of the past tense in l. 17, where the author first brings her earthly identity into the text itself: "My Name was Martha." By referring to herself in the past tense, especially before she has even properly narrated the story of her life, she already implies a distanced perspective on that life and an acceptance of her eventual death, but also a desire to speak to posterity, to leave behind some token of her existence. Through the simple word "was," Moulsworth communicates a remarkably complex set of attitudes and emotions. One word helps create one of the most affecting and poignant moments of her poem, since the very line that introduces her by name also anticipates her prospective demise.

The careful craft of Moulsworth's poem is evident again in her reference to her namesake, the Biblical Martha. She reminds us how "much payne" that Martha took to prepare her home for a visit by Christ, "her guesse" (and, in another nice example of balanced phrasing, "our Sauiour" [ll. 17–18]). Moulsworth might at first seem proud of her predecessor, suggesting their similarity by implying their mutual devotion to God. Yet the allusion ultimately suggests a firm but understated distinction between their conduct. Thus when the Biblical Martha criticized Mary for neglecting her housework, Christ himself reminded Martha of the need to focus on the more important work of personal salvation. Moulsworth tries to internalize this lesson, asking that "God gyue me grace my Inward house to dight / that he wth me may supp, & stay all night" (ll. 19–20). Her balance here is typical: God must first give the grace that will permit Moulsworth to prepare herself for him. Here as elsewhere in her poem, she expresses an ideal of mutual, reciprocal love. Moreover, the balanced pairing of "supp, & stay" similarly epitomizes her style: she desires not simply a dinner guest but a lodger, someone who will not simply be fed but who will feed, someone who will stay with her throughout the long "night" of her present loneliness, her future death, and her ultimate existence in eternity.[8] What might at first have seemed a proud allusion to the Biblical Martha becomes instead a reminder, both to Moulsworth and her readers, to emphasize inner rather than external preparations. Yet while the Biblical Martha had explicitly criticized Mary, Moulsworth nicely refrains from openly chastising the Biblical Martha. Instead, she practices the very lesson Christ preached, focusing on her own spiritual relations with him rather than on unimportant externals or on faulting others. Her subtle invocation and use of the scriptures relating to Martha typify the thematic and stylistic finesse of her entire poem.

Having just beseeched the assistance of her heavenly father, Moulsworth now describes the character and assistance of the earthly father who so greatly influenced her life. In her typically balanced way, she describes him as a man both "of spottles ffame" and "of gentle Birth" (ll. 21–22), but here again the paired phrases emphasize an important distinction. Moulsworth clearly privileges her father's virtue and moral worth over the accidental circumstance of his birth into the gentry. Obviously she values his social standing, but she emphasizes that his reputation depended more on his own "spottles" character than on his family's rank. Indeed, the very phrase "spottles ffame" suggests the balance Moulsworth so frequently achieves: her father's internal worth (or spotlessness) led to his external, public recognition. Similar balance is achieved by juxtaposing verbs when Moulsworth reports that her father "had, & left lands of his owne possession" (l. 23). The pairing once again implies his social status (by referring to the lands he inherited), but it also once again highlights his own talent and character, since he supervised those lands well enough to leave them to his descendants. Moulsworth's father was thus both fortunate and skilled; he owed his prosperity both to lucky circumstances and to wise management.

Yet in addition to being practical and pragmatic, he was also a man of spiritual and intellectual wisdom, and these are the qualities Moulsworth especially stresses. She tells us that "he was of Leuies tribe by his profession" (l. 24)—that is, some sort of clergyman. The reference to "Leuie's tribe" is not a rhetorical indulgence; rather, it allows Moulsworth to emphasize with subtle wit her father's status as a landowner, since the Biblical Levites were a tribe unique in being landless. Here as elsewhere, Moulsworth does not simply cite the Bible in any thoughtless, mechanical fashion; rather, she uses her allusions to give her own phrasing added resonance and meaning. But it is not only the Bible that Moulsworth cleverly echoes; she also glances back at previous phrasing from her own poem. Thus l. 25 opens by describing her father's connection to Oxford University, which is called "his Mother." Both the phrase and its placement look back to l. 21, which had opened by referring to "My ffather." Just as Moulsworth was nurtured and taught by a literal male, so her father was trained and encouraged by a figurative female, an *alma mater* which, "knowenge well his worth / arayd in scarlett Robe did send him fforth" (ll. 25–26). Then, in a shift highlighted by typically parallel phrasing, this reference to Moulsworth's father being sent forth by Oxford is immediately followed by a reference to Moulsworth herself being "brought vpp" by him (l. 27).

Both the shift and the parallel epitomize the poem's consistent emphasis on balance.

The fact that Moulsworth fails to mention her mother or any siblings only accentuates her crucial relations with her father. Perhaps her mother died before Moulsworth could develop much memory of her, and perhaps the same was true of any brothers or sisters. Or perhaps Moulsworth was an only child whose mother had little influence on her life. Obviously these and other possibilities are purely speculative. The important fact for Moulsworth's poem, however, is that she stresses the connection with her father. This emphasis is obviously relevant to the whole poem's thematic stress on her relations with males. Clearly the first of these relations, with her father, had an extraordinary impact on her life and her sense of self. It is typical, again, of the poem's equilibrium that her father, nurtured by "his Mother oxford," then himself nurtured the intellectual and moral development of his daughter, who then in turn calls for the founding of a new university to nurture other women. Behind the entire poem lies an ideal of reciprocal respect and mutual love, and certainly such love seems to have characterized her link with her father. Thus it hardly seems an accident that she mentions first that he trained her up "in godlie pietie" (l. 27), since this phrase suggests their mutual obligations to the heavenly father they shared. Such religious values precede and make possible the more narrowly personal and social characteristics stressed in the next line, where Moulsworth mentions the "modest chearefullnes, & sad [steadfast] sobrietie" her father inculcated (l. 28). Here again balance is important, not only in the pairing of the two nouns but also in the way, for instance, that "modest" modifies "chearefullnes." A sense of poise characterizes Moulsworth's poem as much as it seems to have characterized her view and habits of life.

Equally characteristic, however, is the sudden juxtaposition stressed by the abrupt opening of l. 28, where Moulsworth emphasizes that her father encouraged not "onlie" such traditionally feminine virtues as piety, chearfulness, and sobriety. Rather, "Beyond my sex and kind / he did wth learning Lattin decke [my] mind" (l. 30). The abruptness of this shift is underlined by the equally abrupt opening of l. 31: "And whie nott so?" This phrase simultaneously echoes the opening of l. 28 ("Nor onlie so") while

also balancing Moulsworth's earlier tone of modesty and defer-
ence. Appropriately enough, her challenging question illustrates
precisely the intellectual independence her father sought to in-
still. Paradoxically, the poem reaches one of its most obvious
emotional high points in this passage defending women's access
to the world of reason—a fact that indicates just how much
Moulsworth valued the right to learn.[9] However, the balance
that characterizes the entire poem immediately reasserts itself
in the following clauses, which humorously defuse the anger pos-
sibly implied by the preceding question. By claiming that, after
all, "the muses ffemalls are / and therfore of Vs ffemales take
some care" (ll. 31–32), Moulsworth shifts from a defensive, ac-
cusatory question to a good-natured joke. Yet the joke has a
poignant edge, since it implicitly acknowledges that the figures
supposedly most concerned with feminine achievement are, after
all, merely mythical.

Perhaps this is why the very next lines shift tone once more,
switching from the playful reference to the muses to a much more
serious protest and proposal: "Two Vniuersities we haue of men /
o thatt we had but one of women then" (ll. 33–34). After first toy-
ing with the notion of depending on the imaginary muses,
Moulsworth now gets down to hard practicalities. Typically,
here again her tone is balanced. She keeps her proposal modest:
just "one" school for women is all she requests. Typically, too, her
request balances strong emotion ("o") with a reasoned conclusion
("then"). Moulsworth proposes an innovation that would have
seemed quite radical at the time, but her initial tone seems mod-
estly moderate. Line 34 can be read as an expression of both sup-
pressed anger and genuine anguish, but in either case the emotion
is ballasted by the logic emphasized by the concluding word,
"then." That word implicitly appeals both to her readers' reason
and to their sense of justice, and l. 34 seems all the more effective
for being so carefully balanced, for holding so many tones in ten-
sion.

In a characteristic shift, the tone of the immediately suc-
ceeding lines is less restrained and more obviously assertive. The
parallels in phrasing between ll. 34 and 35 ("o thatt ... then"; "C
then thatt") only emphasize their different moods. Moulsworth
now confidently proclaims that a university for women would cer-
tainly excel both "in witt, and tongs"—a typically balanced

phrase suggesting both native intelligence (wit) and its expression in language. Indeed, she claims that a women's university would "surpasse / All art of men thatt is, or euer was" (l. 36). This is a surprisingly sweeping assertion that suggests both strong assurance and clear frustration. If Moulsworth's language seems a bit boastful or immodest, that fact partly reflects her belief that women have been denied the right to prove their full potential. What might seem arrogant instead suggests a willingness to be challenged, to be put to the test, to be given the opportunity to compete on fair and equal terms. The very feistiness of Moulsworth's tone suggests her eagerness for a chance to submit to exacting standards. Her assertion does not reject the "art of men" but in fact affirms its value. Moulsworth merely insists that women should have the right to test their strengths in free and open competition. Therefore, what might seem boastfulness instead attempts merely to challenge the preexisting, complacent arrogance of men who simply assume their superiority.[10] By making such a provocatively sweeping claim for feminine ability, Moulsworth dares males to put her claim to the test. Then, even if her assertion of superiority proves false, she has still won the larger and most important point: the right to equal education.

The balanced construction of Moulsworth's poem is evident again in the shift to l. 37: "But I of Lattin haue no cause to boast." Moulsworth checks any pride possibly conveyed by l. 36, but she does so in a way that suggests that her pride there was more in the potential of her sex than in her personal accomplishments. Line 37 suddenly drops us from an audaciously imagined future to an unfortunately actual present. Yet Moulsworth's suddenly more modest tone itself seems complicated as soon as we realize that her linguistic shortcomings resulted not from lack of talent but from lack of encouragement. Thanks to "want of vse," she "longe agoe ... lost" her command of Latin. Perhaps the most surprising thing about this passage is its relative freedom from either self-pity or rancor. Moulsworth simply states a fact, and her words are all the more stinging for being so restrained. Her wry marginal comment ("Lattin is not the most marketable mariadge mettall") balances wit, resentment, humor, and pain, and this complicated mix of tones enters the poem itself in ll. 39–40: "Had I no other portion to my dowre / I might have stood a virgin to this houre." The humor of these lines cannot disguise the frustration they also imply; Moulsworth manages to create a tone combining resignation, acceptance, protest, and wit. The very creation of her poem is part of an effort to elude the limits she describes.

Moulsworth's three-fold repetition of the word "virgin" in ll. 40–42 typifies her clever creativity. Her fanciful reference to the powerful but imaginary "virgin Muses" (l. 41) is framed by the all too practical references in ll. 40 and 42, which remind us that in early modern culture, a "virgin" was first and foremost an unattached and thus relatively powerless woman. Although Moulsworth professes "love" for the "virgin Muses" (l. 41), she also realizes that too exclusive a devotion to them would have left her "a virgin to this houre" (l. 40). It is hardly surprising, then, that she claims to "haue longe since Bid virgin life ffarewell" (l. 42). Both lines, with their emphasis on the passage of time, reinforce one of the poem's most important larger themes. In addition, however, the word "ffarewell" suggests both relief at having escaped the real limits imposed on early modern spinsters and, perhaps, also a frank enjoyment of marital relations.

Moulsworth's attitude toward married life exhibits the same balanced combination of idealism and practicality that typifies her entire poem. She expresses affection for the "virgin Muses" while also accepting the need to marry. Indeed, just as ll. 40–42 thrice emphasize the word "virgin," so the succeeding three lines thrice emphasize her three marriages—a detail that once again exemplifies the poem's balanced construction. In fact, similar balance also exists within and between the latter three lines. Thus l. 43 emphasizes the considered action of Moulsworth's "Right hand," which "did holly wedlocke plight," while l. 44 emphasizes her "Left" hand as the object of her husbands' considered actions, since it three times "with pledged ringe was dight" (l. 44). The parallel phrasing of these lines symbolizes the ideal concord and harmony of a successful marriage, and such harmony is suggested again in the symmetrical syntax of l. 45: "three husbands me, & I haue them enioyde." Much is implied by the emphasized verb; "enioyde" simultaneously suggests physical, emotional, and spiritual satisfaction, and thus in all three senses it looks back to the earlier implications of having bade "virgin life ffarewell" (l. 42). Moulsworth's poem manages to suggest that marriage was at once a culturally prescribed role and a source of genuine personal pleasure. The balanced phrasing of l. 45 is then in turn immediately echoed in l. 46 ("Nor I by them, nor they by me annoyde"), which is itself symmetrically constructed. Here as elsewhere, equilibrium reigns.[11]

Such balance is also apparent, for instance, in ll. 47–48. The first line describes Moulsworth's three husbands as "all louely, lovinge all, some more, some lesse." Whereas "louely" demonstrates Moulsworth's complex appreciation of her husbands' attractions, both of body and of character, "lovinge" suggests in turn the affection they displayed. Yet no sooner does she offer this "all"-embracing compliment than she immediately modifies it with the phrase "some more, some lesse." Thus each half of l. 47 is itself balanced, and then both halves are immediately balanced against one another. The result is a complex assessment of her husbands—an assessment that extols their virtues while also hinting at their shortcomings. Moulsworth combines charity and truth, idealism and realism, and here as elsewhere her measured language enhances her credibility. Her tone seems neither cynical nor naive, and her love seems all the more genuine by seeming so mature. Yet the depth of her love is no sooner established than the death of her loved ones is abruptly announced (l. 48). Even here, however, balanced phrasing imposes a shape on loss. Moulsworth immediately shifts from announcing the absence of her husbands (they are "gonn") to stressing her continued affection for them: "their loue, & memorie I blesse." Thus the line ends by emphasizing not so much the loss of love as its transformation.

Having briefly sketched the history of her married life, Moulsworth now proceeds to fill in the details. Not until she was twenty-one years old, she tells us, did she "bind" herself in marriage (l. 50). Her intriguing verb suggests both agency and passivity, the simultaneous exercise and loss of freedom. Thus even in her use of single words, Moulsworth manages a complex balancing act. Balance is also evident in the very next line, which begins with Moulsworth seemingly admitting, "My springe was late" (l. 51). Immediately, however, this apparent concession is withdrawn: it turns out that this is only the subjective opinion of "some . . . thatt sooner loue." What seems to begin as a valid generalization soon stands revealed as the merely parochial and self-interested judgment of others. Both the structure and tone of this line typify Moulsworth's subtle self-assertion and self-con-

fidence. In fact, the next line, beginning with the assertive con-
tradiction "butt," immediately refutes potential critics: "back-
ward springs doe oft the kindest proue" (l. 52). Here as elsewhere
Moulsworth demonstrates a quiet firmness. Just as she had earlier
anticipated and answered presumably male criticism of her
childhood learning (l. 31), so here she responds to presumably
female criticism of her delay in marrying. Moreover, her double
emphasis on spring in ll. 51–52 ties into the whole poem's
encompassing emphasis on the progress of time and on the seasons
of life. Few words in this poem seem wasted; in one way or an-
other, everything fits.

   The thematic emphasis on time already implied by the dou-
ble references to "spring" becomes explicit in l. 53: "My first knott
held fiue yeares, & eight months more." Such precision typifies
Moulsworth's concern with mutability, and this keen awareness
of time passing adds weight to her larger concern with eternity.
Once again balance prevails: Moulsworth seems to have lived
her life fully aware of its duration and various stages, but also
with a sure sense that its moments were unfolding as part of a
larger scheme. She refers very precisely to the exact lengths of
her successive marriages and periods of mourning, but her preci-
sion hardly indicates self-obsession. Rather, it seems a way of
paying tribute to the loved ones with whom she shared her
time—time she seems not to have regarded as trivial or unimpor-
tant. The repeated references to marriage and mourning contribute
to the poem's larger rhythms of relation and separation, birth
and death, love and longing. Our sense of this rhythm is intensi-
fied, for instance, by the fact that two couplets are allotted to
each of Moulsworth's first two husbands, and that each of those
couplets is itself divided into lines dealing first with marriage
and then with widowhood. However, having established this
balanced couplet rhythm in dealing with her first two husbands,
Moulsworth breaks it in dealing with her third.

   Moulsworth's first pair of marriages are called respectively
a "knott" and a "bond" (ll. 53; 55), and her husbands are not de-
scribed, but rather are just mentioned. These patterns change,
however, when she comes to discuss her latest, longest, and pre-
sumably last marriage; here the emphasis immediately shifts
both to her own choice ("The third I *tooke*"; emphasis added)
and to her final husband's traits ("a louely man, & kind"; l. 57).

By describing his traits as she does, she echoes the distinction first asserted in l. 47 between character and behavior, between the sort of persons her husbands were and the ways they treated her ("louely, lovinge"). However, by calling her third husband "louely," she also prepares for the immediately ensuing line: "such comlines in age we seldome ffind" (l. 58). Here Moulsworth demonstrates a typically balanced view: she implies her appreciation of her husband's appearance and of his personality. Such phrasing reinforces the sensual implications of her earlier claim that she had been "enioyde" by her three husbands and had also enjoyed them (l. 45). Her emphasis on her third husband's good looks seems especially poignant since we know that she writes as a widow, now denied the physical presence she still affectionately remembers. Her emphasis on his "comlines" suggests a frank enjoyment of the body in a poem that elsewhere stresses the spirit. Such phrasing typifies the practical, this-worldly element of Moulsworth's character—an element that makes both her poem and her persona seem so completely balanced and sound.

Moulsworth's frank concern with worldly accoutrements is similarly evident in her next lines, which emphasize her third husband's lineage and social standing: "ffrom Mortimers he drewe his pedigre / their Arms he bore, not bought wth Heraulds fee" (ll. 59–60). Clearly this passage expresses some pride in her connection with this man of rank, and clearly, too, Moulsworth is at pains to stress the legitimacy of his (and her) social standing. As in her earlier references to her father's "gentle Birth" and "lands of his owne possession" (ll. 22–23), so here Moulsworth writes not simply as a woman but as a woman of some privilege and status. She rejects some aspects of the patriarchal social system (as when she criticizes the limits it imposes not only on women's learning but also on the value of such learning), but she also shares many of the assumptions that underlie patriarchal thinking.[12] To say this is not to criticize her; she never pretends to be a social radical. Even her call for educational equality does not fundamentally challenge traditional values; instead, it asks only that women also be allowed to imbibe and display such values. It would be naive, anachronistic, and unfair (not to mention pointless) to judge Moulsworth's seventeenth century "feminism" by the standards of a latter day. Her conservative attitudes about questions of class combine with her more assertive attitudes about the rights of women, and the combination illustrates, again, the complicated equilibrium that her poem everywhere exhibits. It is possible, of course, to see such equilibrium as unsteady and rife with contradictions, but it seems best to understand the poem's balance before deconstructing it.

Such balance is obviously intended and evident, for instance, in the immediately following lines: "third wife I was to him, as he to me / third husband was, in nomber we agree" (ll. 61–62). These lines are balanced both in syntax and in sound (especially in the strong "e" sounds stressed in each line's final syllables), and the reiterated emphasis on the idea of "nomber" clearly fits one of the poem's larger patterns. This emphasis is underscored again, for instance, in the next line's reference to the "eleuen years, & eight months" that Moulsworth was able to share with her third husband. She aptly describes this period as his "autume" (l. 64), since it not only ended in his death but also encompassed the natural later stages of his life. With nice subtlety, she omits any reference to winter when describing the passing of his physical life; instead, she prefers to assert that "a second spring to soone awaie it hasted" (l. 64). Her phrasing here nicely looks back to l. 51, where she acknowledged that her own "springe" had been "late." The echo only makes her later phrasing all the more poignant. By describing her husband's death as his "spring," she clearly alludes with Christian confidence to the notion of dying as a second birth, a renewal or resurrection; yet by immediately asserting that his death happened "to soone," she typically balances spiritual confidence with a restrained, wistful expression of pain or regret. The reference to his "second spring" thus seems not an easy, pious cliché but rather a means of coping with her loss.[13]

No sooner does she mention that loss than she shifts, in typical fashion, to a celebration of him and of their union: "was neuer man so Buxome to his wife / wth him I led an easie darlings life" (ll. 65–66). If the first half of this couplet stresses her husband's conduct, the second emphasizes the pleasure Moulsworth herself derived from his behavior. By calling him "Buxome" she manages to suggest both his authority (his graciousness and indulgence) and his voluntary restraint (his humility and compliance with her own desires). Thus even her use of single adjectives displays the equilibrium so typical of her poem. The line that immediately follows may seem to violate such balance, since it seems to emphasize self-assertion ("I had my will in house, in purse in Store"; l. 67). However, this line also implicitly acknowledges the limits, the circumscribed boundaries, of Moulsworth's domain. Her husband allowed her a great deal of authority within the confines of her domestic role, and in this case, at least, Moulsworth seems to have been content with the status dictated by her sexual identity: "what would a women old or yong haue more?" (l. 67). Thus the very passage in which she might seem to assert herself also suggests the limits to her self-assertion.[14] In addition, of course, the phrasing "old or yong" exhibits another kind of balance even as it reinforces the poem's larger concern with the passage of time.

That concern with time is reiterated once more in the next couplet: "Two *years* Almost *outwearinge* since he died / And *yett*, & *yett* my tears ffor him nott dried" (ll. 69–70; emphasis added). Here the reference to her husband's death is no longer fanciful or figurative (as in l. 64's "a second spring"). Rather, Moulsworth's language is now as blunt and unsparing as the mortality she describes. The double emphasis on "yett" not only lends l. 70 a nice syntactical balance, but it also powerfully underscores both Moulsworth's sense of pain and her surprise that her pain continues to be so intense. Her immediate shift from death to birth ("I by the ffirst, & last some Issue had"; l. 71) exemplifies the kind of balanced juxtapositions her poem so often displays, and in fact it seems a nice coincidence that even her child-bearing should have been evenly distributed between her "ffirst, & last" marriages.

However, no sooner does she tell us about her children than she informs us of their loss: "butt roote, & ffruite is dead, wch makes me sad" (l. 72). A single death is emphasized in ll. 69–70, only to be followed immediately by references to multiple births (l. 71), and then those references are themselves immediately juxtaposed with references to the multiple deaths of both "roote, & ffruite" (l. 72). This last phrase clearly looks back to the equally balanced "ffirst, & last" in the preceding line, yet Moulsworth uses the internal rhyme of "roote" with "ffruite" to achieve not only balanced sound but also obvious irony. The rhyme emphasizes the extent of her current isolation; not until this point do we discover that she is not simply a widow, but a childless widow at

that.[15] Given this fact, her claim that the deaths of her hus-
bands and children make her "sad" seems deliberately restrained
rather than inept or trite. The word "sad," of course, reminds us of
the earlier passage describing how her father had attempted to
instill in her a "sad sobrietie" (l. 28), and certainly, in alluding to
her present isolation, Moulsworth must exercise the emotional
self-control her father seems to have prized.

One indication of such self-control appears in the poem's fol-
lowing passage, one of the longest in the work (ll. 73–97). In this
section, Moulsworth details the actual deaths of her husbands
and connects their passings to larger religious patterns and to
broader Christian themes. Thus, she no sooner expresses her sad-
ness at the way death has touched her life than she also at-
tempts to place her experience in a larger context that will help
give it significance and thereby lessen her pain. She begins with
the seemingly paradoxical observation, "My husbands all on
holly dayes did die" (l. 73)—a fact she seems not to have consid-
ered coincidental or meaningless, and one that also fits well with
her poem's whole thematic emphasis on precise points of time. To
a modern secular reader, the deaths of all three of her husbands
on sacred days might seem merely ironic, but Moulsworth seems to
have considered it not only consoling but also symbolic of the
ways in which events in God's universe are not random, chaotic,
or pointless. This notion is immediately reinforced in the next
line, with its typically balanced rhetoric: "Such day, such waie,
they to the Saint[s] did hye" (l. 74). The stress on death in the pre-
ceding line is followed immediately by an emphasis on resurrec-
tion, on salvation, on an escape to a better life. That emphasis, in
turn, is then immediately balanced by a line that stresses quotid-
ian experience ("This life is worke-day euen att the Best"; l. 75),
but then that line itself is followed by another with an off-set-
ting theme: "butt christian death, [is] an holly day of Rest" (l.
76).

The oscillating, qualifying pattern evident in ll. 73–76 typi-
fies the way Moulsworth's whole poem works, its whole empha-
sis on balanced pairs. This emphasis is clear not only in the struc-
tures of lines but in the treatment of individual words and
phrases. Thus, "worke-day" (l. 75) is clearly balanced by "holly
day" (l. 76), and in fact the very reference to "worke-day" is it-
self framed by two references to "holly dayes" (in ll. 73 and 76)

that help place quotidian events in a properly diminished perspective. Similarly, the adjective in the two-word phrase "This life" (l. 75) already implies a heavenly alternative, just as the adjective in "christian death" already modifies and lessens the importance of the noun. Even the opening of l. 76, with its strong emphasis on the conjunction "butt," looks back to the similar opening of l. 72 ("butt roote, & ffruite is dead"). In the second instance, however, the sudden shift signaled by "butt" introduces consolation, not distress. Such equilibrium typifies both the larger structure and the smallest details of Moulsworth's poem.

This sort of balance is evident again, for instance, in the clever repetition and alliteration embedded in l. 77 ("the ffirst, the ffirst of Martirs did befall"), in the related alliteration of l. 78 (St Stevens ffeast to him was ffuneral"), and in the combined repetition, variation, and alliteration of the ensuing couplet ("the morrowe after christ our fflesh did take / this husband did his mortall fflesh fforsake"; ll. 79–80). Given Moulsworth's intense interest in providential and poetic patterning, it hardly seems coincidental that she should stress that her "second" husband died "on a double sainted day," and that he "tooke his happy way" both "to Jude, & Symon" (ll. 81–82). Her reference to "an auncient Story" (l. 83) about St. Simon establishing English Christianity may at first seem digressive, but it allows her to contrast this questionable legend with the certainty of "holy writt" (l. 85). She thus demonstrates some intellectual sophistication even as she underscores her firm faith, and by emphasizing the need of each Christian to "Mayntayne, & ffight for" the faith (l. 86), she contrasts the remote past with the immediate present and juxtaposes the broadly general with the specifically personal. Her recounting of her husbands' deaths thus evolves into a meditation on her own and others' mortality. In her typically balanced way, she assures us that those who "liue, & die" while maintaining the Christian faith "may well / hope wth the Sain^{ts} eternally to dwell" (ll. 87–88). On the one hand, this last phrasing looks back to l. 74, which had stressed how all her husbands "to the Sain^{ts} did hye." However, ll. 87–88 also isolate her accounts of her first and second husbands' deaths, setting off the description of her most recent bereavement. In death as in life, her third husband is subtly distinguished from his predecessors. Moulsworth's account of his passing and of his posthumous fate is far more elaborate, vivid, and emotional than her description of her first two husbands' passings.

When Moulsworth describes her third husband's death as having occurred "in that season wch doth bringe / vppon dead Winters cold, a lyvlie Springe" (ll. 91–92), she effectively plays on a pattern of seasonal imagery that has been building since the poem's very first line. Clearly, too, such phrasing contributes to the even broader theme of passing time that helps organize her entire work. In a similar fashion, juxtaposing the adjectives "dead" and "lyvelie" typifies the poem's balanced phrasing, and all of these traits come together in the equally balanced rhetoric that prophesies a coming moment of literally physical resurrection:

> His Bodie winteringe in the lodge of death
>
> Shall ffeele A springe, wth budd of life, & Breath
>
> And Rise in incorruption, glorie, power
>
> > > [corrin: 15: 42
>
> Like to the Bodie of our Sauiour

Whereas Moulsworth had earlier spoken merely of her own "hope" someday "wth the *Saint*^ts eternally to dwell" (l. 88), she speaks here with far more certainty and assurance in imagining her husband's revival. Her parallel phrasing emphasizes the three verbs "winteringe," "ffeele," and "Rise," the two clauses "lodge of death" and "budd of life," the alliterative nouns "budd" and "Breath," and the three triumphant nouns "incorruption," "glorie," and "power." In addition, this whole passage is framed by references first to her husband's "Bodie" and then to the "Bodie of our Sauiour," so that a projected future resurrection is guaranteed by reference to one already past. Moulsworth's confident handling of poetic details seems to underscore the spiritual confidence she explicitly professes. Although this passage is one of the most obviously heart-felt in the whole poem, it is also one of the most artful and controlled.[16]

Characteristically, Moulsworth immediately juxtaposes this moment of high personal emotion with a shift in subject and in tone. She switches from firm confidence in her third husband's

bodily resurrection to uneasy uncertainty about her exact relations
with him or her other spouses in the afterlife:

> In vayne itt were, prophane itt were ffor me
>
> Wth Sadness to aske wch of theis three
>
> [Matt: 22.18
>
> I shall call husband in ye Resurrection

Such questioning would be "vayne" in the double sense of being fu-
tile and presumptuous, and Moulsworth underscores the point by
rhyming "vayne" with "prophane" to suggest a pride that is also
impious or irreverent. Yet this expression of patient humility is
balanced by the confidence and assurance implied by "shall"—a
word that suggests understated trust that Moulswourth, too, will
participate in the general "Resurrection" (l. 99). Yet such trust
implies less a confidence in her own merit than a faith in God's
mercy.

Moulsworth's confidence in divine grace seems evident, again,
in the way she automatically assumes that "then shall all in
glorious perfection / Like to th'immortal heauenlie Angells liue"
(ll. 100–01). She almost seems to take for granted her future per-
fection (a point nicely implied by the conjunction "ffor" [l. 100],
which gives the notion an air of inevitability). However, this
trust in her own eternal happiness in fact expresses her confidence
in God's love and forgiveness of "all": just as Moulsworth seems to
have regarded herself as blessed in her relations with the impor-
tant men in her life, so she also seems to have imagined God as
another nurturing, loving male. Her serene survey of her past re-
flects her assured anticipation of her future. She seems to have
regarded her life with quiet satisfaction because she also seems
to have felt little fear of death. Given her constant preoccupation
with numbers and patterning, it hardly seems surprising that her
celebration of a future "glorious perfection" should be voiced in l.
100. The number 100 had, of course, long been associated with
plenitude and completion;[17] the fact that Moulsworth prophesies
the achievement of spiritual perfection in her poem's one hun-
dredth line only suggests again how she tries to emulate God's
sense of order in a literary creation of her own.

As that creation winds to its close, Moulsworth subtly echoes
phrasing from earlier in the poem; this tactic gives her poem an

even greater sense of symmetry and completion than it might otherwise have had. Thus her reference to "th'immortall heauenlie Angells" (l. 101) looks back to l. 80, which had mentioned how her first husband "did his mortall fflesh fforsake." Similarly, when Moulsworth says of the angels that they "wedlocks bonds doe neither take nor giue" (l. 102), she reminds us simultaneously of earlier references to her second marriage ("My second bond"; l. 55) and to her third husband ("The third I tooke"; l. 57). By the same token, the very balance of the phrase "neither take nor giue" typifies the symmetries that so strongly characterize Moulsworth's entire poem, and when she refers to the possibility of "knittinge" a potential "fourth knott" (l. 104), she not only plays with the similar sounds of verb and noun but also glances back at her very first marriage ("My first knott"; l. 53). Moreover, the double emphasis on "knittinge" and "knott" nicely prepares for the Biblical allusion called up by the immediately ensuing reference to "A threefold cord" (l. 105), just as the somewhat mysterious reference to "Another Auncient storie" (l. 106) reminds us obviously and deliberately of the earlier reference to "an auncient Story" (in l. 83). In all these ways, Moulsworth demonstrates an explicit attention to her poem's developing structure—an awareness already strongly implied. The poem's pervasive sense of equilibrium is manifested not only in its individual lines, sounds, and phrases, but also in the final shape it displays.[18]

As has just been shown, part of that shape involves the way the poem circles back on itself, picking up earlier words, themes, and tactics and giving them one last airing. Thus her closing reference to "Widowehood" (l. 108) looks back directly to the title with which her poem began ("The Memorandum of Martha Moulsworth / Widowe"), just as her concluding reference to "the Virgins life" (l. 109) directly echoes the phrasing of l. 42 ("I haue longe since Bid virgin life ffarewell"). Similarly, it hardly seems surprising that a poem punctuated by powerful questions (as in ll. 31 and 68) should also close with one ("whie should I / then putt my Widowehood in jeopardy?"; ll. 107–08). If Moulsworth's first question had displayed frustration at the lack of proper schooling for women ("And whie nott so?"; l. 31), and if her second had in contrast displayed satisfaction at her treatment by her third husband ("what would a women old or yong haue more?"; l. 68), her third displays a different kind of satisfaction altogether. As both her life and her poem worked toward their endings, Moulsworth seems to have felt content with the autonomy her widowhood allowed her. Whereas her first and second questions seem to have been directed outward (first at male and then at female readers), her third query seems to have been directed mainly at herself, and perhaps secondarily at society in general. Although a question in the strict grammatical sense, line 108 has the effect of resolving doubts rather than of raising them.

It seems fitting that a poem so much concerned with recounting the past should end by emphasizing the present and future—what Moulsworth nicely calls "the Meane tyme"; l. 103. In the course of her poem, this poet expresses both loss and hope, both regret and anticipation, but her final note is one of contentment, of acceptance of the here and now ("the Virgins life is gold, as Clarks vs tell / the Widowes siluar, I loue siluar well"; ll. 109–10). How appropriate it is that her work should end with a few last balanced oppositions (between gold and silver, between virginity and widowhood, and between the opinions of others and an opinion of her own). Yet how appropriate, too, that the poem's very last words should stress the resolution of such opposites. It hardly seems surprising that these last words express such equanimity and self-assurance, such subtle self-assertion. Nor does it surprise us that Moulsworth ends by emphasizing not simply "loue," but a love and self-respect so firmly felt. She finishes her poem as she seems to have lived her life—in a spirit not of resignation but of acceptance. She does not simply acquiesce in her fate; instead, she willingly embraces it. In her final words as in her entire poem, she conveys a tone of perfect balance.

It is difficult to finish Moulsworth's poem without feeling respect for both its artistry and its author. The work displays both craft and freshness, both conscientious design and simple dignity. Its tone is complex but never chaotic or confused, and Moulsworth's achievement—as a poet and person—seems all the more impressive considering the constraints she faced as a writer who was also a woman. However, one needn't apologize for the poetic quality of her work: it stands as a worthy and accomplished text, firmly embedded in concrete historical contexts which it nevertheless in many ways transcends.[19]

Notes

1. Germaine Greer notes that numerous "women who versified in their youth destroyed the evidence when they came to riper years and lost their privacy by marrying." See her "Introduction" to *Kissing the Rod: An Anthology of Seventeenth-Century Women's Verse*, ed. Germaine Greer, Susan Hastings, Jeslyn Medoff, and Melinda Sansone (New York: Farrar Straus Giroux, 1989), 6. The destruction of women's verse makes Moulsworth's poem all the more valuable, and it is additionally interesting that Moulsworth wrote her poem at the end of her life, after the deaths of her husbands, during a time when she presumably enjoyed greater personal autonomy.

2. Similarly, Sara Mendelson notes that "a common trait displayed by female diarists was the urge to impose some comprehensible order upon the fortuitous incidents that made up their lives"; see her essay "Stuart Women's Diaries and Occasional Memoirs," 186.

3. In *The Paradise of Women*, Betty Travitsky notes that the only discernible difference between Renaissance women's prose and poetry is that sometimes the latter displays a "more conscious striving for artistic effect" (18). Certainly this seems true of Moulsworth's "Memorandum."

4. In *The Paradise of Women*, Betty Travitsky reports that most of the religious poetry written by the women she has studied is "intensely partisan," a fact that makes Moulsworth's balanced, generally tranquil tone all the more noteworthy.

5. Germaine Greer notes that the "pious of both sexes were often required to keep a spiritual diary," and one way of viewing Moulsworth's poem might be to see it almost as a summation or epitome of her spiritual life. See Greer's "Introduction" to *Kissing the Rod*, 12.

6. See, for instance, J.C.J. Metford, *Dictionary of Christian Lore and Legend* (New York: Thames and Hudson, 1983), 240.

7. Sara Mendelson notes that the "providential interpretation of life's accidents which moulded contemporary spiritual diaries" could help "transform an outwardly dull and unhappy life into scenes of high drama, punctuated by hairbreadth escapes

from death or damnation.... Many of these daily balance sheets seem to have had a cathartic as well as an interpretive function.... Sometimes this confessional purpose of the diary could lead to exaggerated expressions of guilt for minute lapses, so that the author could be sure she had settled her spiritual account for the day." See "Stuart Women's Diaries and Occasional Memoirs," 186–87. Moulsworth's poem, of course, is not a diary, but its tone of calm assurance and lack of spiritual hyperbole are nevertheless two of its most striking features.

8. It may be worth noting at this point Mendelson's observation that some Stuart women's diaries reveal "an emotional involvement with God which goes far beyond the allegorical relationship that clerics presumably had in mind. Among certain women with no husband or an extremely unsatisfactory one, some sort of erotic transference seems to have taken place." See "Stuart Women's Diaries and Occasional Memoirs," 195. Moulsworth's phrasing might be read as suggesting a hint—but only a hint—of such transference; here as elsewhere her phrasing is understated and subtly suggestive.

9. In *The Paradise of Women*, Betty Travitsky suggests that secular manuscript writings by women may indicate a "high degree of interest" in writing and a "hard-won erudition" (90).

10. Linda Woodbridge notes that in fact formal defenses of women were more numerous in the Renaissance than outright attacks, although she tends to regard both defenses and attacks as mainly literary gamesmanship; see *Women and the English Renaissance: Literature and the Nature of Womankind, 1540–1620* (Urbana and Chicago: University of Illinois Press, 1984), 44; 111; 129. Moulsworth's poem suggests that some women, at least, took the controversy seriously. For a collection of highly relevant texts, see Katherine Usher Henderson and Barbara F. McManus, eds., *Half Humankind: Contexts and Texts of the Controversy about Women in England, 1540–1640* (Urbana and Chicago: University of Illinois Press, 1985). See also Joan Larson Klein, ed., *Daughters, Wives, and Widows: Writings by Men about Women and Marriage in England, 1500–1640* (Urbana and Chicago: University of Illinois Press, 1992).

11. Helen Wilcox notes that Lady Anne Halkett's memoirs were structured around her own relations with the three different

men to whom she was romantically attached. See her essay "Private Writing and Public Function: Autobiographical Texts by Renaissance Englishwomen," in *Gloriana's Face: Women, Public and Private, in the English Renaissance*, ed. S.P. Cerasano and Marion Wynne-Davies (Detroit: Wayne State University Press, 1992), 47–62; for the fact about Halkett, see 50.

12. For a similar case, see Angeline Goreau's comment on Anna Maria van Schurman (1607–78), a Dutch woman who in 1641 "published a treatise arguing that women ought to be allowed a classical education." Still, Goreau concludes her discussion by noting that van Schurman "is an interesting example of the way in which a woman could challenge certain social restrictions that applied to her sex, and yet defend equally restrictive assumptions at the same time—either explicitly or implicitly." See *The Whole Duty of a Woman: Female Writers in Seventeenth Century England* (Garden City, N.Y.: Doubleday, 1985), 164–65. For a similar point concerning Shakespeare's presentation of women, see Linda Woodbridge, *Women and the English Renaissance*, 216–17. See also the concluding argument by Margaret George in her book *Women in the First Capitalist Society: Experiences in Seventeenth-Century England* (Urbana and Chicago: University of Illinois Press, 1988), 254.

13. In her "Introduction" to *Kissing the Rod*, Germaine Greer comments that the "attempt to versify on religious themes was a discipline intended to focus concentration on well-worn pious truisms" (12). Part of the interest of Moulsworth's poem is that she manages to make such truisms seem vital, both to herself and to her readers.

14. Helen Wilcox reports that "generally Renaissance women risked a distinctly unwanted reputation by entering the public sphere, particularly in areas less well sanctioned for feminine activity than charity and nursing." She notes, however, that it "was quite common for a woman to manage the financial and even legal affairs of a household...." See "Private Writing and Public Function," 53.

15. In her "Introduction" to *Kissing the Rod*, Germaine Greer reports that "perhaps 45 per cent of middle- and upper-class women died before reaching the age of fifty and more than half of them of complications of pregnancy" (11). These data make the

fact that Moulsworth survived all her husbands and children seem even more striking.

16. In her "Introduction" to *Kissing the Rod*, Germaine Greer comments that among "the genres a literate gentlewoman might be expected to master was the farewell to her husband about to be widowed. Such a poem was intended to display deep love and fortitude, with control and resignation mimetically conveyed by lucid, balanced syntax uncontorted by demands of rhyme or metre" (11). Moulsworth's poem displays many of the qualities Greer specifies, yet her work is a "farewell" to her husbands written by a widow who has survived them all.

17. See, for instance, George Ferguson, *Signs and Symbols in Christian Art* (New York: Oxford University Press, 1954), 278.

18. In her "Introduction" to *Kissing the Rod*, Germaine Greer cautiously suggests that certain "syntactic patterns" tend to characterize much of the verse written by early modern women. These include "endless chains of clauses which may be related back and forwards with equal justification, rather than a hierarchy of main clauses with obvious subordinates" (9). Meaningful ambiguity is sometimes a feature of Moulsworth's phrasing, but in general she seems to have been quite concerned with the clarity of her poem's structure.

19. In her "Introduction" to *Kissing the Rod*, Germaine Greer comments that much religious poetry by early modern women "was intended to remain private; most of the women who versified as part of a religious exercise had no interest in communicating their individual experience to outsiders; the poems ... are usually laborious and dull" (13). Moulsworth may or may not have hoped that her poem would be published; some of her phrasing (such as the call for equal education) certainly suggests an interest in influencing readers. In any case, Greer's final comment gives us a standard for assessing the literary merit of Moulsworth's poem, which seems accomplished and thoughtful rather than "laborious and dull."

Chapter 2

HISTORICAL CONTEXTS

A standard claim concerning Renaissance women is that their lives were structured chiefly by their relations with men. According to this claim, early modern women generally moved through a predetermined pattern of social roles—living first as daughters, then as wives, and finally often as widows. Even variations from this pattern helped confirm the norm: a spinster, after all, was simply an unmarried woman; a nun was a bride of Christ. One virtue of studying the lives of Renaissance women in terms of this larger pattern is that the pattern itself is not an anachronistic imposition. It seems, in fact, to have been a standard way for early modern women themselves to understand and express their own experiences.[1] Certainly this seems true of Martha Moulsworth. Her highly structured poem is organized quite clearly in terms of her successive roles as daughter, wife, and widow, yet her poem also indicates the actual complexity of such roles and how they might be subject to change or even challenge.[2]

In Moulsworth's case, the challenge, of course, mainly involves the issue of womens' education; her poem is one of our earliest records indicating that "ordinary" women themselves were beginning to chafe at and protest against the limits on their right to learn.[3] The fact that Moulsworth's protest seems not to have been widely known, and that it was never issued in print, hardly diminishes its importance. Indeed, the relative privacy of Moulsworth's vigorous objections may suggest not only the subtle ways in which intelligent opinion was beginning to evolve, but also both the constraints on and movement toward new habits of thought and behavior. Fascinating as a complex work of art, Moulsworth's poem is equally interesting as a complicated reaction to—and expression of—the various roles that women could play in early modern culture. By looking at Moulsworth's poem against the background of recent scholarship dealing with issues of women's education, and by examining her poem in light of Renaissance attitudes toward daughters, wives, and widows, we can better appreciate the special interest of her "Memorandum" as both a work of art and an historical document.

I. Women and Education

It is easy—perhaps too easy—to generalize about Renaissance attitudes toward women. "The Renaissance" itself, of course, is merely a handy label for an enormously long and complex period that not only witnessed many debates, but that has also generated many more disputes among the scholars who have subsequently studied it. In fact, the subject of women was itself a frequently debated topic during the Renaissance, and this is only one reason why we should be careful about making broad or sweeping claims about the period's "typical" views. In the end, Renaissance culture consisted of individual persons whose individual attitudes were likely to have been shaped by particular experiences.[4] Moulsworth herself is one such case, and perhaps the most sensible way to approach her poem historically is to view it against the spectrum of possible ideas and behavior available to her. Then we will be in a better position to appreciate the special features of her "Memorandum" and its part in the complex mosaic of Renaissance life.

For most readers, the most interesting aspect of Moulsworth's "Memorandum" is likely to seem its explicit call for higher education for women:

> Two Vniuersities we haue of men
> o thatt we had but one of women then
> O then thatt would 'in witt, and tongs surpasse
> All art of men thatt is, or euer was. (ll. 32–36)

Historical investigation suggests that Moulsworth's call was indeed unusual. Standard histories of Renaissance women cite various views from the period about the goals and limits of women's education, but the phenomenon of an English woman herself calling so early and unambiguously for women's universities seems to have been rare if not unique. In 1639, it is true, a book entitled *The Complete Woman* generated controversy by arguing strongly that women were just as capable as men of being educated. Translated from a French work written by Jacques Du Bosc (first published in 1632 as *L'Honneste Femme*), *The Complete Woman* was never reprinted in England. Joan Larson Klein suggests that this was "in part perhaps because of the uncertainties of civil war, in part perhaps because of the controversy it generated over its elevation of women to a position of equality with men" (257). According to Klein, Du Bosc's book "certainly appeals more to twentieth-century sensibilities than does any other [Renaissance] conduct book" she cites (258), yet even Du Bosc seems silent on the subject of university training for women. Moulsworth, then, would seem to enjoy the distinction of being one of the first English females to tackle this topic—and to tackle it so bluntly—in a poem.[5] Both her "Memorandum" and Du Bosc's book seem part of the same general mind-set, the same general movement of thought, but Moulsworth's poem is all the more intriguing for having been written by an English woman herself at such an early date.[6]

Moulsworth, of course, was neither writing nor thinking in a vacuum. As Ralph A. Houlbrooke notes,

> From the sixteenth century onwards, a succession of writers, in England as elsewhere, claimed that women's mental abilities, properly developed, were the equal of men's. Women themselves complained of their exclusion from education, devised by men in order to secure their own continued domination, in both *The Woman's Sharpe Revenge* of 1640 and in Hannah Woolley's *The Gentlewoman's Companion* (1675). The conservative feminist Mary Astell argued in *A Serious Proposal to the Ladies* (1697) that women's improvement was frustrated by bad education, custom, and the low and wrong aims proposed to them, especially the attraction of men as an end in itself. Better-educated women would indeed be more interesting companions for their husbands, but above all better fitted for their paramount responsibility, the religious education of their children. So while she sought to free women from the tyranny of fashion and custom, Astell insisted that the family was their

proper sphere; they had no business with "the Pulpit, the Bar or *St. Stephen's Chapel....*" (99)

Thus, as Houlbrooke and many other scholars make clear, Moulsworth was not alone in chafing at the educational limits imposed on women.[7] Significantly, however, all the sources Houlbrooke cites post-date Moulsworth's poem, and the gaps in time are often quite long. Moreover, even the "feminists" Houlbrooke does quote make claims that seem modest compared to Moulsworth's call for a female university, and in fact Houlbrooke concludes by remarking that "Despite their reiterated demand for better female education, none of the English feminist writers of our period [1450–1700] proposed a major extension of woman's role" (99). Moulsworth, then, would seem to be the exception who proves the rule. Her claim that the achievements of university-educated women "would in witt, and tongs surpasse / All art of men thatt is, or euer was" (ll. 32–36) seems remarkably forthright and sweeping; she seems to have set no limit on how fully women might develop their minds if given half a chance.[8]

Reason's Disciples, Hilda L. Smith's study of seventeenth-century English feminists, also suggests the unusual significance of Moulsworth's call for higher education. Moulsworth is nowhere mentioned in Smith's book, yet Smith provides valuable evidence that helps us appreciate the importance of Moulsworth's poem. Although almost all most of Smith's "feminists" come from the latter half of the century, she argues that one of their core beliefs was the assumption "that women were men's intellectual equals whose potential had been thwarted by exclusion from institutions of higher learning" (4), and she shows that a few of these post-Restoration feminists "argued for the establishment of a woman's college, advanced secondary schools for girls, and the furtherance of learning by women in their own homes" (4). Like Houlbrooke, she also emphasizes the importance of Mary Astell—noting, for instance, that in 1694 (Houlbrooke had said 1697), Astell's *Serious Proposal to the Ladies* "continued the demand" (made by a few other recent writers) "for quality education for women, even calling for the establishment of a women's college" (14). Astell's public declaration was indeed important, even if her proposals were rather modest (as Houlbrooke claims). Yet Moulsworth's "Memorandum" preceded Astell's book by more than sixty years. The point is not to deny Astell any credit, but rather to indicate that the ideas she expressed may have begun to take root, per-haps even in a fairly radical fashion, among ordinary women decades earlier than has previously been assumed.

Smith argues, in fact, that it was the "gap in educational op-portunities between men and women [that] most angered the femi-nists. The educational opportunities were limited for women at both ends of the social scale" (20).[9] Although some women estab-lished informal contacts with university scholars, "it would sim-ply have been unthinkable for them to have attended institutions of higher education as students" (Hilda Smith 21). However, as Moulsworth's poem clearly indicates, the idea of university edu-cation for women was indeed quite thinkable—if still very im-practical—fairly early in the century, and at least one relatively ordinary woman had thought about the topic quite seriously. As a matter of fact, the data Smith presents may help to explain why Moulsworth and other women were becoming increasingly frus-trated with the limits imposed on their right to learn. Smith con-tends that while the educational status of Englishwomen re-mained relatively stagnant, "educational opportunities for En-glishmen were expanding in two different directions during the early and mid-seventeenth century" (21). She reports that there was "signficant growth in numbers of university students," and that this growth "took place both among poorer students ... and among the children of the gentry" (21). Indeed, "the number of students gaining first degrees grew sixfold between the 1520s and the 1620s, the period of fastest growth in Oxford's entire history, and advanced degrees increased proportionately" (22).[10] From such facts Smith concludes that although "feminists born after 1660 did not experience these patterns of change, they were equally or even more conscious of the central social truth they represented: universities were open to men who had less ability and were from lower social strata than many of the women who were systematically denied an advanced education" (23). Because Smith focuses mainly on feminists from later in the century, she suggests that the "largest growth in the numbers of men entering the universities and the greatest educational agitation occurred before the seventeenth-century feminists wrote" (22). Yet this statement now seems too categorical: Moulsworth's previously unpublished poem provides us with the response of an intelligent woman whose life coincided rather precisely with Smith's pe-

riod of "educational agitation." Indeed, Moulsworth lived specif-
ically during the era of the unprecedented expansion of educa-
tional opportunities for men that Smith describes. Mary Astell,
in the last decade of the century, may have been one of the first
English women to call publicly for equal access to higher educa-
tion, but Martha Moulsworth, at least as early as 1632, seems to
have been one of the first not only to entertain the idea seriously,
but also to give it vigorous expression.[11]

Of course, by 1632 the topic of women's education had been a
much-discussed matter for many decades, owing in large part to
the influence of the English humanists of the early sixteenth cen-
tury.[12] Most histories of Renaissance English women note the im-
pact of humanist thought, although they often disagree about its
precise effects. Thus Retha M. Warnicke, in her classic study of
Women of the English Renaissance and Reformation, notes that
Thomas More, "Because he established a school in his home for
his three daughters, one son, and other youth, ... is usually recog-
nized as the first Englishman to extend humanist training to
women" (17). More's daughter Margaret became "the perfect fe-
male humanist: a devoted daughter, a virtuous and obedient
wife, an educator of her children, and [an] esteemed scholar" (25)
who even published a work under her own name (albeit a transla-
tion from her father's friend Erasmus). Although by doing so "she
had already exceeded even her father's view of the proper
bounds of women's activity" (25), Margaret More provided an ob-
vious precedent for the intellectual aspirations of a woman like
Martha Moulsworth.

II. Women as Daughters

The close attachments that both Margaret More and Martha
Moulsworth felt to their fathers, and the real interest both fa-
thers seem to have taken in their daughters' educations, are par-
ticularly intriguing. In fact, it was almost inevitably to her fa-
ther that a girl with serious educational ambitions would have
to turn for guidance. Or rather, it was almost inevitably upon her
father's largesse that such a girl would have to depend
Moulsworth's intelligence is impressive, but it might never have
been nurtured had she been born to a different father. Thus, ever

when transcending the traditional limits imposed on females, women such as Moulsworth inevitably depended on men. The deep appreciation Moulsworth expresses for her father seems genuine, but it also suggests the limits of her freedom as a woman.[13] She probably would never have attained anything approaching her potential without his assistance or acquiescence.

The precedent Thomas More established in educating his daughters seems to have been followed by other Renaissance fathers. Warnicke argues that Henry VIII, "who was lauded as the patron of humanism from his succession to the throne, took a personal interest in the education of [Princess] Mary, his only legitimate child at that time" (33). Similarly, Warnicke also notes that "it was largely the male relatives of the second generation of women humanists who hired their instructors and who made most of the decisions concerning the content of their academic training" (107–08). Mothers, in fact, often ignored or opposed their daughters' education (Warnicke 108), perhaps because they felt threatened by it. This fact may help explain why Moulsworth nowhere mentions her own mother, whom she might have been expected to extol. Moreover, the precedent established by More and other male humanists may even have provided a direct inspiration to Moulsworth's father—who was, after all, himself a learned man presumably familiar with humanist ideals. If More had won prestige for having raised a learned daughter, perhaps Moulsworth's father shared similar aspirations. In any event, the achievements of both Martha Moulsworth and Margaret More depended not only on innate talent but on good fortune—particularly on the good fortune of having been born into a comfortable family headed by a thoughtful and generous male.[14] Moulsworth, of course, clearly recognizes and acknowledges her luck. Her devotion to her father is plain, but it also poignantly testifies to the particularly dependent status women endured in Renaissance culture. Without her father's influence and inspiration, we might never have had her poem. Paradoxically, it was partly thanks to the impact of such males that male dominance began to wane. Moulsworth's father at once reinforced, exemplified, and helped undermine and modify his culture's patriarchal traditions.

In this and in other ways, Moulsworth's experiences illustrate many trends discussed by Elaine V. Beilin in her book *Re-*

deeming Eve: Women Writers of the English Renaissance. Beilin
argues, for instance, that "Tudor theorists were at best ambiva-
lent and at worst prohibitive when considering how women might
use their education" (3). Chastity was the womanly virtue most
often stressed by humanist educators, particularly by the highly
influential Juan Luis Vives. In Beilin's words,

> Instead of the free exploration of his world that would
> lead a man to develop judgment and the virtues suitable for
> public life and action, a woman would receive pieces of in-
> formation about the world, filtered through her preceptor
> whose goal was to make her a chaste wife, mother, and if it
> so happened, widow.[15]

Moulsworth's life obviously fits this pattern in many ways,
but her strong call (even near the end of such a "chaste" life) for
equal access to education indicates some real dissatisfaction with
such enforced cultural norms. In her own small way, Moulsworth
exemplifies the fear felt by many Renaissance opponents of
women's education, who claimed (according to Beilin) "that once
a woman began to learn, men would no longer be able to choose her
reading lists or prevent her from preferring the pen to the needle"
(11). Although Moulsworth had enjoyed only a brief taste of the
kind of classical education the humanists championed (albeit
mainly for men), she never forgot its savor. By treating his young
daughter with some measure of intellectual respect, Mouls-
worth's father had helped awaken appetites that never quite
died. Those yearnings eventually led even so chaste a wife,
mother, and widow to express genuine exasperation with the lim-
its she had had to endure.

On the whole, however, Moulsworth's poem demonstrates
(and perhaps was even intended to demonstrate) the standard
humanist claim that a certain level of education could only en-
hance a woman's virtue and companionability. Richard Hyrde,
for instance, had argued in favor of teaching women classical lan-
guages precisely on the grounds that "such studies would improve
any mind, male or female, and that whereas a woman's mind
might wander into evil while only her fingers were busy with
sewing, if she learned Greek and Latin, her mind would be fully
occupied with good" (Beilin 15).[16] Indeed, Moulsworth's
"Memorandum" almost seems designed to preempt potential

charges that an intellectually sophisticated woman would prove anything less than virtuous; Moulsworth protests against the limits placed on women's right to learn, yet she simultaneously exemplifies the companionable ideals that caused some humanists to defend female learning. Her interest in acquiring classical languages goes hand-in-hand with her deep interest in reading scripture, and in this sense she epitomizes the religious emphasis so characteristic of other women writers of this period.[17] Beilin notes, for instance, that between 1545 and 1560, fifteen published works of religious prose were either written or translated by women, and she argues that

> when these few women assumed the roles of teacher, preacher, and witness to the faith, they created the vital link between women's traditional spirituality and their developing literary vocation. The very existence of these works indicates the increasing importance for women of recording their religious experiences and beliefs themselves. (48)

Moulsworth fits this pattern: the self-expression her poem embodies could be justified, in part, because it also expressed the religious values sanctioned by her culture.[18] She speaks for herself, but she also speaks for a patriarchal religious system—a system she seems genuinely to have embraced. Just as Moulsworth's relationship with her indulgent earthly father gave her an access to learning denied to many other girls, so her obedience to her heavenly father permitted her to speak as she might not otherwise have done. Her Christianity thus both limited and permitted her mental development and self-expression. Christian doctrine subordinated women in many ways, but it also offered them an authoritative voice and a claim to spiritual (if not social) equality.[19] In fact, Beilin's claims about the writings of the female religious authors she discusses might just as easily apply to Moulsworth's poem:

> The scriptural basis of women's writing in this period manifests itself both in the content and the style of their works. Like Anne Askew and other Reformers, they think Biblically, and their writing modulates, often imperceptibly, between Biblical quotations or references and their own words. Almost without exception, they write in the

"Protestant plain style," an unornamented, Biblical English aimed at a universal audience. In some cases, their vivid, colloquial expression suggests that these writers would gladly have joined their brethern in the pulpit. (51)

Although Moulsworth's style is not exactly plain (in fact, she seems to have striven consciously for complicated artistic effects), nonetheless her manner is neither fervent nor pompous; she writes with the restraint and authority of a person confident that her basic beliefs give her a right to speak. She seems intent on demonstrating that an educated woman would not threaten but would in fact strongly endorse the fundamental values of her culture. Moreover, the fact that she shows herself so committed to Christian ideals would presumably have helped create sympathy for her desire for access to even greater knowledge.[20] Moulsworth's argument on behalf of a women's university may sound radical (and in some senses it obviously was), but there seems little doubt that the school she envisions would not fundamentally challenge the larger religious assumptions of her time. In this sense, her "Memorandum" offers both an explicit call for, and an implicit demonstration of, the merits of feminine learning. Her poem quietly but firmly refutes anyone who might claim that women were intellectually handicapped or unsophisticated, even as it affirms many of the most cherished values of her culture. Through this combination of the conservative and the unconventional, the poem once again demonstrates its essential balance and moderation.

The fact that Moulsworth never forgot her father's early interest in her education testifies to the important impact that parents—and particularly male parents—could have on their children's lives. Most Renaissance children were strongly affected by their fathers' views and actions, but this was especially the case with daughters. They had far fewer prospects for independent futures, and far more limited legal standing, than did their male counterparts. Boys, after all, could at least hope to attend universities or enter the professions, and eldest sons, of course, enjoyed special privileges of inheritance and familial authority. Girls, however, were usually thought of primarily as wives in training; they would someday simply trade one dominant male for another. Moulsworth's father taught her to embody all the virtues that might eventually appeal to a respectable

husband ("godlie pietie / ... modest chearefullnes, & sad sobri-
etie"; ll. 27–28), but his added efforts to cultivate her knowledge
of the classics were pragmatically pointless.[21] Her marginal note
claiming that "Lattin is not the most / marketable mariadge /
mettal" (l. 38) is typical in the way it balances cynical bluntness
with wry humor; it betrays Moulsworth's own awareness that
adolescent girls in her culture were viewed largely as commodi-
ties of exchange. The size of a woman's dowry had long been the
chief factor affecting her prospects for marriage, and Moulsworth
was only acknowledging the facts of life when she said of her
skills in Latin, "Had I no other portion to my dowre / I might
have stood a Virgin to this houre" (ll. 39–40).[22]

III. Women as Wives

Chastity itself was considered perhaps the prime virtue in a
Renaissance woman, but chastity unsupported by a healthy
dowry might well prove insufficient in attracting a mate. As
Margaret L. King observes, "From the instant of her birth, the
prospect of a dowry loomed large over the female: she repre-
sented potential loss rather than potential gain" (26). Even near
the end of her life, decades beyond her girlhood, Moulsworth
never forgot this fact. In this respect as in many others, her poem
helps buttress many of the points recent feminist scholars have
made about the position of Renaissance women. Yet the poem not
only confirms such scholarly claims but also gives us the chance to
know and (perhaps more important) to *feel* how such facts af-
fected one woman's actual existence. Moulsworth's explicit refer-
ence to the marriage market mixes resentment with realistic ac-
ceptance. Here as in other aspects of her life, she seems to have
been able to imagine alternative styles of thinking and living
while still playing the cards she had been dealt.[23]

Thus, despite her sardonic observations about the marriage
market, Moulsworth seems to have derived real satisfactions
from her own relations with her three husbands. In fact, of all
the roles she played, the role of wife was by far the most impor-
tant, since it occupied the greatest part of her maturity. Her poem
is valuable historically simply as a piece of data about how one
woman enacted and interpreted that role, for, as Joan Larson

Klein observes, we have little access to the period's "private thoughts or to much information about actual relations between husbands and wives, all of which are ephemeral by their very nature" (x). Moulsworth's poem gives us the reactions of one real and intelligent woman to the institution of marriage, and the fact that she was married three times only increases the inherent interest of her work.

Ralph Houlbrooke argues that "Christian thought about the relationship between husband and wife, grounded on certain key Scriptural texts, underwent no major change" during the period he studies, and Moulsworth's extended account of her lengthy experience with marriage would seem to confirm his claim. Certainly she seems to have had the same expectations concerning all three of her husbands, and she also seems to have judged their conduct by roughly similar standards. If she enjoyed greater autonomy in her third marriage than in her first two, that fact may have derived as much from her own greater maturity and experience as from her third husband's liberality. He could afford to give her greater freedom because she already possessed years of practical wisdom. As Houlbrooke sensibly notes, "The actual location of power in the relationship of husband and wife depended upon a number of variables, of which individual character and temperament are the hardest to quantify" (101). Moulsworth's poem nicely illustrates this point, yet it seems worth noting that even in her relatively liberal relationship with her third husband, the initiative toward greater mutuality seems to have been taken by him ("was neuer man so Buxome to his wife / wth him I led an easie darlings life"; ll. 65–66).[24] Moulsworth seems to have realized that in marrying this particular husband, just as in having been born to her particular father, she had been unusually lucky. In both cases the individual characters of specific men had had profound effects on her life.

It is this emphasis on individual circumstances and character that again contributes to the value of the "Memorandum" as a piece of history. Whereas published writings from Moulsworth's period often tend to portray women in largely symbolic terms (as extreme instances of either virtue or vice), the self-portrait embodied in Moulsworth's poem is refreshingly complicated and nuanced. Her "Memorandum" tells us a great deal not only about her own life, but about what life could actually be like for any woman and wife during her time. For instance, although Renaissance wives were theoretically and theologically consigned to subordinate positions in their relations with their husbands, Moulsworth's poem illustrates a point made by Joan Larson Klein, who notes that the further that contemporary texts "move away from theological assumptions about woman's place and the nearer they come to describing the actual conditions of women's lives, the less emphasis we find on notions of women's subordination, inferiority, and frailty" (x).[25] Certainly in her dealings with her third husband, Moulsworth seems to have regarded marriage as a genuine partnership—one in which a wife could exercise a good deal of autonomy. Her relations with Bevill Moulsworth, in fact, seem to have exemplified many of the ideals extolled in the standard marriage homily, which stressed marriage as "a perpetual friendly fellowship" (Klein 13). The homily speaks of marriage as a "godly knot" (Klein 14), and it refers to God's help and his holy spirit, through which husbands and wives should so "knit their minds together that they be not dissevered by any discord or division" (Klein 15). Moulsworth's poem, of course, plays with similar language of knots and knitting, and she found and valued in her third husband the kind of mate the homily extols: one who would "use measurableness and not tyranny" and who would "yield some things to the woman" (Klein 16).

However, Moulsworth also seems intent on disproving through her own words and manner the homily's immediately following sentence, which claims that "woman is a weak creature, not endued with like strength and constancy of mind" (Klein 16). Balance, restraint, and self-control were probably genuine features of Moulsworth's personality, but they may also have been features she wanted to stress in order to counter the widespread male stereotype of women as weak-minded and inconstant.[26] Moulsworth seems to have done her best, in her poem as in her life, to exemplify the highest ideals associated with Renaissance wives, and in her third husband in particular she seems to have found a mate who valued her as a nearly equal partner. She seems to take for granted the Protestant idealization of marriage as opposed to celibacy, even to the point of wondering about the survival of marriage after death. Moreover, her explicit reference to having "enioyde" her husbands (and to having been "enioyde" by them; l. 45) suggests a frank acknowledgment of the physical side of marital relations. According to Ralph Houlbrooke, standard Christian doctrine echoed St. Paul in teaching that "each spouse's body belonged to the other, and the satisfaction of the marriage debt was second only to procreation among the legitimate motives for sexual intercourse" (103).[27] Indeed, in her delicate reference to the mutual enjoyment of marriage, Moulsworth seems to endorse Erasmus's argument that marriage consisted "not only in the benevolence of the mind, but also in the conjunction of the body" (Klein 82). In fact, in her general attitudes she seems to have shared Erasmus's opinion that of all earthly conditions, "nothing is neither safer, neither quieter, neither pleasanter, neither amiabler, neither happier, than the wedded life" (Klein 85).

This was not true, of course, of all Renaissance marriages; even standard exhortations and conduct books frankly admitted that marriage was often an unpleasant experience, especially for women. The standard marriage homily, for instance, conceded that it was a "miserable thing" when couples were "of necessity compelled to live together which yet cannot be in quiet together," yet it also admitted that such frustrating circumstances were "most customably every where to be seen" (Klein 15). Indeed, one value of Moulsworth's poem lies in the evidence it provides that "companionate" marriages, rooted in mutuality and reciprocity, were not only valued during the Renaissance but were also sometimes achieved.[28] Of course, achieving a happy marriage was particularly important for women; the marriage homily itself bluntly acknowledged that females "must specially feel the griefs and pains of their matrimony in that they relinquish the liberty of their own rule" (Klein 18). Similarly, the compiler of a comprehensive legal text bluntly admitted, "I know many an honest woman more repenting her hasty marriage ere she was wooed than all the other sins that ever she committed" (Klein 39). Moulsworth seems to echo this sentiment when she mentions that

> Vntill my one & twentieth yeare of Age
> I did nott bind my selfe in Mariadge
> My spring was late, some think thatt sooner loue
> but backward springs doe oft the kindest proue
>
>   (ll. 49-52)

Moulsworth seems to have been both willing and able to delay her first match, and perhaps this fact helped account for the apparent success of the marriages she did make. Her initial delay, like her intervening periods of widowhood, gave her a greater opportunity to develop as an individual and thus to exercise, both before and during marriage, some measure of autonomy.[29] By resisting cultural pressures to marry too soon, she seems to have been able to strike a balance, not only enjoying a longer than usual period of freedom but also exemplifying the chaste ideal articulated by writers such as Vives. He had argued that adolescent women were "giuen unto most lust of the body" (Klein 107), and had claimed that it was "not comely for a maid to desire marriage, and much less to show herself to long therefore" (Klein 111). When she did marry, Moulsworth seems to have "enioyde" her husbands, but she also seems to have enjoyed and appreciated being single. Here as in other respects, her poem displays its typical equilibrium.

The language Moulsworth uses to describe her first wedding is worth noting. When she mentions that until she was twenty-one she did not "bind" herself in marriage, her verb is interesting for various reasons. Clearly it echoes the common idea (voiced in the marriage homily) of matrimony as a permanent bond—and thus as one that should not be entered into lightly. In this sense the word suggests Moulsworth's maturity, good sense, and rational conduct. If her poem can be believed, she seems to have approached her first marriage with the same intelligence and judgment she continually displays throughout the "Memorandum" itself.[30] Moreover, the verb "bind" also suggests some degree of conscious, deliberate choice; it implies, in some measure, a voluntary union. This point seems important, since the extent of free marital choice during this period has been a subject of historical debate. Moulsworth's phrasing supports the arguments of those who contend that some women in her society could exercise at least some measure of individual autonomy, both in selecting a mate and in determining a proper time for marriage. Yet the verb "bind" also inevitably implies a loss of freedom, and, as we have already seen, contemporary commentators were quite blunt in acknowledging that for women, more than for men, marriage involved some sacrifice of liberty. As Vives himself admitted, "there is much weariness in marriage and many pains must be suffered. There is nothing but one that shall cause marriage to be easy unto a woman, that is, if she chance on a good and wise husband" (Klein 111). Moulsworth seems to have regarded her third husband, in particular, as such a mate.

Of course, as Katherine Usher Henderson and Barbara F. McManus remind us, the contemporary emphasis on the "sovereignty of the husband did not imply that the wife had no autonomy; it meant that she had only the degree of autonomy that he saw fit to give her" (78). Moulsworth's third husband seems to have been more generous than her first two in this respect, but her poem suggests that she was never really dominated or oppressed by any of her mates. In this sense her "Memorandum" may perhaps reflect another observation made by Henderson and McManus: "Accounts of Continental visitors to England in the period suggest that the married Englishwoman had more freedom than her counterpart in other countries" (77). Certainly Moulsworth seems to exude throughout her work a healthy self-respect—an attitude perhaps first encouraged by her father and then nurtured during her relations with the three other men most important in her life, especially her last husband. In fact, her poem seems to take for granted many of the most common assumptions made about marriage during the period in which she lived: that the foundation of a solid marriage lay in religious faith (Klein 14–15), that women would appreciate and respond to courteous treatment (Klein 16), that a cooperative wife could enjoy a fair degree of independent power (Klein 17), that husbands and wives each had special duties to perform (Klein 21), and that by honoring her husband, a woman also honored God (Klein 18). The marriage homily had stressed that "when either parts do their best to perform their duties the one to the other, then followeth thereon great profit to their neighbors for their example's sake" (Klein 20). Seen in this light, Moulsworth's "Memorandum" functions not merely as a private account of her individual experiences, nor simply as one person's summary of her existence (written partly with God in mind), but also as an account of a Christian life that might benefit any friend or descendant who happened to read it. As far as we know, Moulsworth took no steps actually to publish her poem, but the care she lavished on it plainly suggests that she hoped it would be read.

Anyone who did read Moulsworth's poem could not help but notice how clearly if implicitly the work exemplifies (and in some cases subtly modifies) many of the ideals championed by Renaissance advocates of worthy wives and marriages. Moulsworth's reasonable and balanced tone, for instance, makes her seem anything but a stereotypical shrew. Any criticism of her husbands' behavior is only lightly insinuated, never stridently voiced. She seems to display the patience and consideration that so many moralists valued in wives, but she hardly seems utterly subservient or lacking in self-respect. She seems neither to have acted as a slave nor to have been treated as one; instead she exemplifies the companionable qualities of intelligence and good will that the moralists prized. She seems to have been chaste but not frigid, pious but not humorless or fanatical, obedient but not servile, and quietly thoughtful rather than utterly mute. Her intelligence seems to have fortified rather than undermined her virtue, and her learning seems to have buttressed her faith rather than weakened it. She shows herself a "reasonable creature," capable of being counselled (Klein 128), and she shows no inclination toward thoughts or acts that might have been perceived as "vain," "childish," or "superstitious" (Klein 129). Her style is "simple, not affectate nor ornate" (Klein 130), but it is hardly artless or unsophisticated. She shows no signs of vanity about her appearance or clothes (Klein 133), and she seems to have proven herself a competent manager of household affairs (Klein 208–11). In all these ways she seems to have embodied many of the ideals most frequently advocated for Renaissance women.

It is striking, in fact, how closely Moulsworth seems to exhibit many of the feminine virtues celebrated in Richard Braithwaite's conduct book *The English Gentlewoman*, published in London in the year just before her poem was written. Braithwaite, for instance, considers civility a principal virtue in any woman, and certainly this is a trait that Moulsworth's poem everywhere exemplifes (Klein 234). He argues that the ideal woman should display reason and virtue and should consider it "her highest honor to promote the glory of her maker" (Klein 241). Yet she should not be humorless or strident; he hopes, instead, that "the modesty of her method" will "beget admiration" (Klein 234). She should be knowledgeable enough to deliver judgments on many topics (Klein 236), yet she should not be vain about either her intelligence or her appearance: she should be "serious in her advice, temperate in her discourse, discreet in her answers" (Klein 236). Like Moulsworth when she compares herself to the Biblical Martha, Braithwaite's gentlewoman should show an interest in moral self-vigilance and self-correction, and she should teach more by example than by precept (Klein 236). She should prefer "the incomparable liberty of her mind before the mutable formality of a deluded age" (Klein 237), and she should desire to be "complete in the exercise of goodness" (Klein 237). "A cheerful modesty is her best complement" (Klein 237), and she should display piety and religious values (Klein 237). She should be generous, and "howsoever she might boast of descent, her desire [should be] to raise it by desert" (Klein 237). She should scorn "to entertain one thought below herself or to detract from the glory of that house from whence she came" (Klein 238)— an admonition worth remembering when one considers Moulsworth's evident pride in the family backgrounds of her father and third husband. In Moulsworth's mind, such backgrounds probably not only conferred status but also implied certain standards of ethical conduct and moral aspiration.

Of course, one of the most valued ways for any Renaissance wife to contribute to her family's honor was to produce heirs (preferably males) and to raise them as good Christians.[31] For this reason, one of the most poignant aspects of Moulsworth's poem is her extremely brief reference to the deaths of the children she did bear to her first and third husbands. Her reticence on this subject—she mentions merely that the topic "makes [her] sad" (l. 72)—might be explained in various or even contradictory ways. Her brevity, for instance, may reflect the deep pain the loss of her children caused her, or it may support the contention of some historians who argue that Renaissance children were so likely to die that their parents could not afford to make great emotional investments in them. Perhaps Moulsworth's children, like so many others, succumbed at very early ages; thus she may not have had much opportunity to become closely attached to them as individual personalities. When she imagines her relations in the afterlife with other people, she specifies her husbands, not her children, and her own mother is nowhere mentioned in her poem. The absence of any children at the time

Moulsworth wrote probably increased her sense of personal isola-
tion and may in fact have provided her with one real incentive to
pen her "Memorandum": lacking surviving children, she perpetu-
ates her life and personality in a poem. Certainly the legacy she
imagines when she calls for a woman's university, and the legacy
she creates by writing this work, is a legacy of the mind rather
than of literal physical offspring. Her poem allows her to leave
at least something of herself behind, and she lavishes the kind
of careful attention on writing it that many mothers might have
lavished on a living child.[32] Lacking the solace or emotional
"comfort" that many Renaissance parents seem to have desired
most from their surviving offspring (Wrightson 114), Moulsworth
instead turns her attention to the male figures in her life with
whom she *had* bonded most closely: her father, her husbands,
and God. She seems to find some solace or comfort not only in
thoughts of them, but also in the act of writing.

IV. Women as Widows

By the time she sat down to write, Moulsworth was enduring
again a role with which she had already become familiar—the
role of widow. It was an experience common to many women of her
day. According to Henderson and Usher, "the duration of the av-
erage marriage in Renaissance England was short, for the major-
ity of marriages were interrupted by the early death of either
husband or wife. Available evidence suggests that the median
duration of a first marriage in England in 1600 was twenty-two
years" (75). Moulsworth's own first marriage, of course, was far
more brief: her husband died in less than six years, and in fact
neither of her subsequent two marriages lasted much longer than
a decade. The periods of widowhood that intervened between her
first and final marriages varied from one year to nearly four, and
at the time she composed her "Memorandum" she had been a
widow again for almost another two. These periods of forced sep-
aration from the role of wife obviously caused Moulsworth pain,
but they may also have increased the sense of independence her
poem displays. In particular, the three years and eight months
she spent unmarried after the death of her second husband must
have given her a taste of autonomy that may have enhanced her

sense of self-reliance.[33] Of course, the decision not to marry for a fourth time, announced at the end of the poem, may partly have been a forced choice: many influential voices in her culture spoke against remarriage (Klein 120), and her advanced age may also have made Moulsworth an unlikely marital candidate.[34] Yet she had already twice shown a willingness to ignore cultural strictures against remarriage, and the reason she explicitly offers for refusing to remarry suggests that she now valued her independence and feared losing it through an unlucky match: "whie should I / then putt my Widowehood in jeoparady?" (ll. 107–08). Her logic, in this case, seems to have been rooted as much in pragmatism as in any concern for religious teachings or social prejudices. Ironically, the relative autonomy she had enjoyed with her third husband seems to have made her unwilling to risk marrying a less liberal mate.[35]

Contemporary sources and subsequent scholars concur that the role of widow was not entirely unfortunate in Renaissance culture. Moulsworth thus had good reason to worry about putting her "Widowehood in jeopardy." Margaret L. King, for instance, surveying the experiences of European widows, remarks that "if her husband died first, a woman was sometimes able to acquire significant economic independence, particularly in the north of Europe and in the middle classes. In these instances, widows could dispose of wealth themselves, or bear it advantageously" to subsequent husbands (56).[36] Significantly, Moulsworth's poem nowhere suggests any sense of strong financial need; thus her tone of admirable self-reliance may have been due as much to favorable economic circumstances as to qualities inherent in her character.[37] Her third husband in particular seems to have enjoyed some social and economic prominence, and presumably he left her a comfortable legacy. In any case, at the time she composed her "Memorandum," she seems to have felt no great financial pressure to remarry.[38] In fact, it is possible that generous inheritances from her first two marriages helped make her an attractive partner for her third mate—the one who then in turn granted her so much independence that she was wary of chancing another match.[39] Near the end of her life, having now been thrice married and thrice widowed and having enjoyed a third husband willing to entrust her with an unusual degree of freedom, Moulsworth seems to have appreciated a fact reported by King: "'No wife could at-

tain the social freedom available to some widows'" (56).[40] A con-
temporary legal writer could even bluntly ask, "Why mourn you
so, you that be widows? Consider how long you have been in sub-
jection under the predominance of parents, of your husbands; now
you be free in liberty, and free ... at your own law" (qtd. in King
50). St. Jerome himself had described widowhood as an "occasion
of freedom," involving (in King's words) "liberation from a phys-
ical and psychological enslavement to a husband" (58). However,
the conclusion of Moulsworth's poem gives this idea a slightly
different twist: her third marriage had been so liberal and so far
from "enslavement" that she was reluctant to risk the disap-
pointment a fourth match might well have posed.[41]

According to contemporary English law, a daughter or wife
was always legally subject to her parents or husband; even vows
to God made by such women could be disavowed by their parents
or mates. "But the vow of a widow or of a woman divorced, no man
had power to disallow of, for her estate was free from control-
ment" (Klein 50). A widow, then, enjoyed a kind of legal and in-
tellectual autonomy rare for women in early modern culture, and
Moulsworth's recognition of this fact may help to account for the
balanced tone she takes toward her widowed condition. Many
women, in fact, seem to have mourned hardly at all when their
husbands died, and Vives had written that "the greatest token
that can be of a hard heart and an unchaste mind" was for "a
woman not to weep for the death of her husband" (Klein 119). Yet
he had also noted that "there be too kinds of women which in
mourning for their husbands in contrary ways do both amiss: that
is, both they that mourn too much and those that mourn too lit-
tle" (Klein 119). In this respect as in so many others, Mouls-
worth's poem displays a kind of perfectly balanced emotional
equilibrium: she mourns for her husbands, but she does not mourn
excessively. She exemplifies the counsel, voiced by Vives, that
"a good widow ought to suppose that her husband is not utterly
dead, but liveth both with life of his soul, which is the very life,
and beside with her remembrance" (Klein 119).[42]

In fact, Moulsworth's poem itself may be seen, in one sense, not
only as a summing-up of her own life but also as a lasting tribute
to her mates and a response to the kind of thinking that led an-
other writer to advise widows "constantly to live out the residue
of their days in a devout remembrance of their dear husbands de-

parted" (Klein 55).[43] Moulsworth seems determined to "live and
do so as she shall think to please her husband, being now no man
but a spirit purified and a divine thing" (Klein 120). Indeed, as
her poem shows, even after his death a husband's influence on his
wife did not end; in fact, Vives urged a widow to regard her de-
ceased husband as "her keeper and spy, not only of her deeds, but
also of her conscience" (Klein 120). She should therefore conduct
herself as her husband would have wished, always remembering,
too (in the words of Richard Braithwaite), "to give examples of
her blameless life to such as hear her instructions attentively.
For she ought to be as a glass to young maids" and reflect Chris-
tian virtue. Although free in some senses, a widow still had obli-
gations to her deceased husband(s), to the values of her patriar-
chal culture, and above all to God.[44]

Although Moulsworth obviously mourned for her husbands
and remembered them with genuine affection, she finally seems
to have decided to seek solace in her link with a far more impor-
tant male: her heavenly father. She was undoubtedly religious
throughout her life, but the loneliness of widowhood may have
made her especially conscious of her dependence on God. She
seems to have followed the advice of the contemporary legal
theorist who urged that a widow should "learn to cast her whole
love and devotion on him that is better able to love and defend
her than all the men in the world" (Klein 50). God, of course, was
at once a more present and more absent figure than any of the
other males in her life had been. He was not an inescapable
physical fact, and he could not directly or immediately enforce
his decrees in quite the way that an angry husband could. He was
always with her, of course, but his influence on her everyday
thoughts and actions depended greatly on how strictly her
conscience (influenced, to be sure, by church doctrine and other cul-
tural pressures) chose to interpret his commands. In addition,
Moulsworth could always assume that God had her best interests
at heart—that his power over her would always be exercised for
her ultimate benefit. This was a fact she could not inevitably
take for granted in her relations with any flawed human male, no
matter how well-intentioned he might be. Thus in her relation-
ship with God, as in her links with her father and her third hus-
band, Moulsworth seems to have experienced and appreciated not
only affection and protection, but also a good deal of personal

dignity.[45] The self-respect instilled by her early experiences with her earthly father seems to have been reinforced by her faith in God. The confidence with which she speaks is a confidence largely rooted in the assurances of Christian belief.

In all the roles Moulsworth played—whether as daughter, wife, mother, widow, and even writer—her experiences seem to have been shaped, both for good and for ill, by her status as a Christian. The freedoms she enjoyed, as well as the restrictions she faced, were rooted largely in the assumptions of a culture grounded in a patriarchal faith. However varied her relations with various men, Moulsworth seems everywhere conscious that her most important connection was with God. Both the liberties she enjoyed and the limits she experienced must ultimately be seen in the context of a universe ruled by a powerful, threatening, but ultimately benevolent male.

Notes

1. Sara Mendelson remarks, for instance, that early modern "women themselves appear to have been very self-conscious about passing through" the distinct stages of "virginity, marriage, and widowhood." See "Stuart Women's Diaries and Occasional Memoirs," 191.

2. Barbara J. Todd notes, for example, that "through the early modern period widows came to be less likely to remarry." See her essay "The Remarrying Widow: A Stereotype Reconsidered," in *Women in English Society 1500–1800*, ed. Mary Prior (London and New York: Methuen, 1985), 54–92; for the quoted passage, see 83. Prior's volume is exceptionally helpful and relevant to the focus of this chapter, as are the following other texts: Katherine Usher Henderson and Barbara F. McManus, eds., *Half Humankind: Contexts and Texts of the Controversy about Women in England, 1540–1640*; Ralph A. Houlbrooke, *The English Family: 1450–1700* (London and New York: Longman, 1984); Margaret L. King, *Women of the Renaissance* (Chicago and London: University of Chicago Press, 1991); Hilda Smith, *Reason's Disciples: Seventeenth Century English Feminists* (Urbana, Chicago, and London: University of Illinois Press, 1982); Retha M. Warnicke,

Women of the English Renaissance and Reformation (Westport, CT: Greenwood Press, 1983); and Keith Wrightson, *English Society: 1580–1680* (New Brunswick, NJ: Rutgers University Press, 1982).

3. Patricia Crawford notes, for instance, that although "it has been argued that women in the seventeenth century were not sufficiently conscious of themselves ever to write or speak for themselves as women, their own statements suggest that they were forced to write for publication because they knew that their experiences as women were different from those of men." See her essay "Women's Published Writings 1600–1700," in *Women in English Society 1500–1800*, ed. Mary Prior (London and New York: Methuen, 1985), 211–82. For the quoted passage, see 211–12.

4. As Betty Travitsky memorably puts it, "in a sense, there were as many Renaissance Englands as there were individual inhabitants of England during the Renaissance." See her "Introduction: Placing Women in the English Renaissance," in *The Renaissance Englishwoman in Print: Counterbalancing the Canon*, edited by Anne M. Haselkorn and Betty S. Travitsky (Amherst: University of Massachusetts Press, 1990), 3–41, esp. 8.

5. In *The Paradise of Women*, Betty Travitsky suggests that "there was as yet no Marie du Gournay in England to call for the equal education of men and women and for the right of women to engage in any work, as the French writer did in her *Egalité des hommes et des femmes* (1622). The earliest, even faintly comparable, argument by an Englishwoman appeared in 1640 in a pamphlet entitled *The womens sharpe revenge*" (93). Moulsworth's poem, although unpublished, predates the latter work by eight years.

6. For another example of a woman (but not an Englishwoman) calling for classical education as early as 1641, see Angeline Goreau on Anna Maria van Schurman in *The Whole Duty of a Woman*, 215. Patricia Crawford notes that early modern women "were aware that there were certain rules for different kinds of discourse, and they felt uneasy at not knowing them. Even in the religious sects, where inspiration was to replace formal learning, women resented their exclusion from university education"; see "Women's Published Writings 1600–1700," 215. However, both of the examples she cites in support of this contention date from con-

siderably later than Moulsworth's poem, which makes the latter's stance seem all the more original. Incidentally, it could be argued that in her poem Moulsworth attempts to display her mastery of a particularly challenging kind of discourse and to exhibit a particularly "masculine" ability at precise and conscious ordering. Perhaps in this way she was reacting against the cultural stereotype of the excessively emotional and intellectually erratic woman.

7. In *The Paradise of Women*, Betty Travitsky notes that "once women were allowed and even encouraged to develop their minds, it was inevitable that some would be moved at least to ponder the larger inequities of their lives" (11). Angeline Goreau argues that women writers of the seventeenth century "generally deplored their lack of training in arts and sciences and looked back with envy to the 'golden age' of Tudor England, when a woman's learning was seen as one of her attractions" (1). See also Margaret George, *Women in the First Capitalist Society*, 233–50.

8. Of course, it could be argued that Moulsworth could afford to be so forthright because she may have been writing mainly for herself. Concerning those who actually published, for instance, Patricia Crawford notes that some "women responded to negative attitudes to their writing by showing anxiety about their sexual identity. Some believed that by acting in ways not sanctioned by the ideology they risked their femininity.... Women who published anonymously may betray ambivalence about their sexual identity, suppressing their gender in order that their words might be taken seriously." See "Women's Published Writings 1600–1700," 219–20. On the other hand, Moulsworth's forthrightness on this issue seems entirely in keeping with the calm but sturdy character she displays elsewhere in her poem.

9. In *The Paradise of Women*, Betty Travitsky comments that the "thinking of the early English humanists concerning women proved most helpful to women of the privileged classes, some of whom became highly educated through private tutelage; for, while the humanists did not intend to restrict their ideas to the privileged, they developed no program of schooling for the common people. Toward the end of the sixteenth century, however, humanist educators were advocating schooling for women" (6–7). Angeline Goreau comments that most "—in fact, nearly all—of

the women who published either literary or other sorts of texts (philosophical, polemical, etc.) during this period [the seventeenth century] lodged some kind of complaint about the inadequate instruction usually afforded their sex." See *The Whole Duty of a Woman*, 7.

10. See also the data cited by Angeline Goreau in *The Whole Duty of a Woman*, 5.

11. Angeline Goreau notes that the Dutch woman Anna Maria van Schurman, who also called for improved education for women, nevertheless wrote "in the awkwardly stiff form of a 'logic exercise,' an expedient, one can't help feeling, to which the author resorted in order to provide a protective shield against attack." See *The Whole Duty of a Woman*, 164.

12. In *The Paradise of Women*, Betty Travitsky contends that by "advocating a change in the quality of daily life, and by asserting the spiritual-intellectual-moral equivalency of men and women, Christian humanism laid the foundation for the equal education of men and women" (235). On the other hand, Angeline Goreau argues that "the influence of this passion for educating women was much less extensive than legend might suggest"; see *The Whole Duty of a Woman*, 1. Travitsky herself elsewhere notes that "while humanists and Protestant theorists paid startlingly new attention to women's minds, they did so to uplift women's personal spirituality and to equip them better for their traditional, domestic roles." See her "Introduction: Placing Women in the English Renaissance," in *The Renaissance Englishwoman in Print*, 24. In fact, Lisa Jardine is "tempted to conclude ... that humanist education conveniently distracted able women from any studies which might have led them to notice that change was opening up possibilities for emancipation in social and political fields." See *Still Harping on Daughters: Women and Drama in the Age of Shakespeare* (Totowa, NJ: Barnes and Noble, 1983), 52. Similarly, Marilyn J. Boxer and Jean H. Quataert assert that the "Reformation did not markedly transform women's place in society, and the reformers had never intended to do so." See their "Overview" in *Connecting the Spheres: Women in the Western World, 1500 to the Present*, ed. Marilyn J. Boxer and Jean H. Quataert (New York and Oxford: Oxford University Press, 1987), 31.

13. In her essay on "Stuart Women's Diaries," Sara Mendelson notes that although "unmarried young women comprise the smallest group" of the diarists she studied, "it seems clear that, despite continual subordination to parents or guardians, maidenhood represented the most carefree and enjoyable of the three female conditions" (191).

14. Germaine Greer, in her "Introduction" to *Kissing the Rod*, notes that throughout the seventeenth century, "the proportion of women who could sign their names to legal documents remained low, in the region of 11 per cent" (2).

15. See Elaine V. Beilin, *Redeeming Eve: Women Writers of the English Renaissance* (Princeton: Princeton University Press, 1987), 6. Angeline Goreau pragmatically notes that since "the aristocracy's chief means of consolidating and perpetuating power and wealth was through arranged marriage, the undoubted chastity of daughters was a crucial concern." Partly for this reason, "Legally, a woman's chastity was considered the property of either her father or her husband"; see *The Whole Duty of a Woman*, 9–10.

16. Patricia Crawford notes that in the seventeenth century, "Virtually all women were ignorant of Latin, the language of professional and theological discourses. Educated men did not expect women to participate in their discussions." See "Women's Published Writings 1600–1700," 215.

17. Germaine Greer, in her "Introduction" to *Kissing the Rod*, notes that although most women could read their Bibles, writing remained an unusual activity (4)—facts which make Moulsworth's accomplishments all the more remarkable.

18. Germaine Greer, in her "Introduction" to *Kissing the Rod*, notes that even to "the end of the [seventeenth] century and long after, religion remained the only area in which female wit could safely exericse itself in print but some impetuous young women failed to grasp the fact" (16).

19. Lisa Jardine suggests the importance of "facing up to the inevitable equivocations which attend even the most liberal patriarchal discussion of the appropriate place of women in religion, education, and the home"; see *Still Harping on Daughters*, 39. Interestingly, Sara Mendelson notes that "a high proportion of female diarists were the wives, daughters or patronesses of

clergymen.... Clergymen's families, like clergymen themselves, were more literate than the average for their social class, and the wife's facility in self-expression was apt to be matched by her husband's ability to edit and publish her manuscripts." See "Stuart Women's Diaries and Occasional Memoirs," 189. These facts seem obviously relevant to Moulsworth's experience.

20. Sara Mendelson comments that "There are reasons for suspecting that a substantial amount of non-devotional writing [in manuscript] may have disappeared" since "editors from the seventeenth to the nineteenth centuries exhibited a marked preference for female piety." See "Stuart Women's Diaries and Occasional Memoirs," 188. Perhaps Moulsworth's poem survived partly because of its religious emphasis.

21. Patricia Crawford provocatively asks, "if women were educated in Greek and Latin, how could their thoughts be confined? Latin and Greek may not have made men radical, but they were marked out as male territory." See "Women's Published Writings 1600–1700," 229. Crawford's question and comment help us appreciate more fully the radicalism of Moulsworth's challenge to limited education. Theodora A. Jankowski argues that the "discourse of humanism, which purported to validate a woman's intellectual capacities and raise her social standard by educating her 'like a man,' paradoxically helped to denigrate women by creating 'monstrously' intellectual creatures who did not fit any acceptable discourses of womanhood." See *Women in Power in Early Modern Drama* (Urbana and Chicago: University of Illinois Press, 1992), 48.

22. Angeline Goreau asserts that even "in exceptional cases when particularly enlightened parents sought to 'improve' their daughters by education, they often manifested extreme anxiety as to the effects this learning might have on the attractiveness of their offspring." See *The Whole Duty of a Woman*, 4. Later she notes that "as the seventeenth century progressed, it became more and more the practice to send daughters to the increasing number of boarding schools that were being established. The curriculum of these 'academies' for young ladies laid emphasis on practical rather than intellectual achievement, as marriage was to be the future occupation of the great majority of their scholars" (6).

23. Sara Mendelson reports that "Once marriage was in prospect, ... young women often entered a tense and anxious period." Some of the diarists she studied "noted their unwillingness to abandon their liberty." Mendelson comments that marriage "could represent a major trauma for women, and various sources reveal that they regarded it as the crucial turning-point in life." See "Stuart Women's Diaries and Occasional Memoirs," 191–92.

24. Lisa Jardine suggests that Protestant moralists "maintained that moderation in marital relations made the task of authoritative control of wives simpler"; see *Still Harping on Daughters*, 43.

25. In support of this suggestion, see Linda Woodbridge, *Women and the English Renaissance*, 135.

26. Thus Samuel Torshell in 1645 recommended the "calm-constant-watchful-modest-composed disposition" as the most excellent for ladies; see Angeline Goreau, *The Whole Duty of a Woman*, 42.

27. On this issue, see also Margaret George, *Women in the First Capitalist Society*, 205–18.

28. Sara Mendelson reports that from the evidence provided by twenty-one married female diarists, "there were fifteen loving and companionable marriages, and six unsatisfactory marriages." See "Stuart Women's Diaries and Occasional Memoirs," 193.

29. Sara Mendelson provides documentary evidence of "the importance that contemporaries attached to giving all parties the opportunity to consent" to marriage. See "Stuart Women's Diaries and Occasional Memoirs," 193.

30. Charlotte F. Otten emphasizes Renaissance views of the disorder love could cause—views that make Moulsworth's calm, measured tone in describing her romantic involvements all the more noteworthy. See Otten's edited collection, *English Women's Voices, 1540–1700* (Miami: Florida International University Press, 1992), 128.

31. In *The Paradise of Women*, Betty Travitsky asserts that "the evolution of the woman in English Renaissance society became centered in the woman as mother, since only this facet of the woman underwent an approved rise in autonomy at this time" (9).

32. In *The Paradise of Women*, Betty Travitsky notes that "the option of a religious career as a nun or abbess was closed to women in Protestant countries like England, so that their effective choices for a lifetime vocation were greatly limited. The woman's role in the home became increasingly the only, but at the same time the newly elevated, role for women" (237). At the time Moulsworth wrote, of course, she was no longer playing the role of either wife or mother, which may help to explain her interest in poetic self-expression.

33. Barbara Todd notes that the one "group that was more likely to remarry were widows with young children"; see "The Remarrying Widow: A Stereotype Reconsidered," 68. This fact may perhaps help explain Moulsworth's several remarriages as a young woman and her decision not to remarry when childless at age fifty-five.

34. Barbara Todd, in "The Remarrying Widow: A Stereotype Reconsidered," reports a growing trend to penalize widows in various ways for remarrying (74), and she notes that playwrights of the period treated remarrying widows, particularly elderly ones, as stock comic characters (54). Moulsworth's poem therefore assumes added interest and importance, because both her tone and her explicit statements contradict many of her culture's stereotypes concerning remarrying widows. She speaks out not only as a woman or as a widow, but as a thrice-married widow at that. The dignified tone of her poem is perhaps an unconscious reaction against the comic stereotype.

35. Barbara Todd, in "The Remarrying Widow," notes that "the independent widow was an anomaly.... The woman heading her own household contradicted the [conventional] patriarchal theory; the ungoverned woman was a threat to the social order" (55). Moulsworth, typically, manages to strike a balance: despite her independent thinking about equal education, she conforms to her culture's expectations in most other important ways, and thus her poem ultimately seems far less threatening than if it had focused on the educational issue alone.

36. Barbara Todd, in "The Remarrying Widow," notes that in England, after "about 1570 an interesting change began to occur, first in the wills of men of greater wealth and social standing, and later, in the seventeenth century, of men of all social ranks.

Rather than depending on the good offices of a future husband, these testators made certain that their wives should take none of their wealth into a new marriage by inserting a penalty withholding or reducing the wife's share of the estate if she remarried" (73).

37. On this point, Sara Mendelson's observations about widows seem relevant. She notes "two contrasting patterns." In the first, "some women apparently came into their own when the toils of child-bearing and the rigours of wifely subordination were over. They had earned the independence and resources to do as they pleased.... For other women, widowhood not only deprived them of a beloved companion but plunged them into a sea of economic difficulties." See her essay "Stuart Women's Diaries," 198–99.

38. Barbara Todd, in "The Remarrying Widow," cites evidence "that through the early modern period widows came to be less likely to remarry" (83).

39. Barbara Todd, in "The Remarrying Widow," suggests that "the remarriage of widows was becoming increasingly less common in the seventeenth century when the [comic] stage widows flourished" (56).

40. On this point see also Betty Travitsky, *The Paradise of Women*, 91.

41. Moulsworth's poem thus challenges the conventional stereotype, reported by Barbara Todd (in "The Remarrying Widow"), "of the early modern widow as a woman who anxiously sought a husband at any cost" (55).

42. In her essay "The Remarrying Widow," Barbara Todd notes that "it was the widow who did remarry who was criticized; for, as men realized, the remarriage of any widow confronted every man with the threatening prospect of his own death and the entry of another man into his place" (55).

43. On the deep attachment many widows felt for their husbands, even after remarrying, see Barbara J. Todd, "The Remarrying Widow," 79.

44. In "The Remarrying Widow," Barbara Todd suggests that it "might be supposed that because of the legal disabilities of marriage early modern widows preferred extramarital liaisons,

and that this was the source of the many contemporary notions about widows' sexual promiscuity. Yet little evidence has ever been adduced to indicate that English widows were particularly likely to transgress sexual rules" (77).

45. Contrast the experiences and feelings of other women noted by Patricia Crawford in "Women's Published Writings: 1600–1700," 219. On this point, see also Angeline Goreau, *The Whole Duty of a Woman*, 9.

Chapter 3

THE POEM AS AUTOBIOGRAPHY

A poem as carefully crafted and thoughtfully phrased as Moulsworth's "Memorandum" would be of interest if it came from the pen of any Renaissance writer; the fact that in this case the writer was a woman only enhances the fascination of the work. This is particularly true considering the fairly radical stance the poem adopts toward women's education. However, what makes Moulsworth's poem still more interesting is its clear autobiographical focus. In this sense the poem is significant not only as a work of art and an historical document, but also as one of the earliest contributions to a kind of writing that was still relatively recent and fairly rare during the period when Moulsworth wrote. Moulsworth deserves attention, therefore, not simply as a skillful Renaissance writer, or as an early female author of secular verse, or as an innovative thinker on education, or even as a simple source of historical information, but also as one of the earliest authors of autobiography in Renaissance England, and as one of the very few women from this period to practice this kind of writing.[1]

The autobiographical impulse might seem an inevitable part of human nature, and in fact James Olney, whose work has contributed so much to a better understanding of autobiography as a literary genre, sees that impulse as rooted in a basic desire for order and coherence that sparks all human creativity (3). For this reason, Olney argues, every human creation is autobiographical in some sense (5), and history itself can be seen as autobiography writ large (49). Every human act is a statement, an assertion, about the self who acts. Yet the impulse actually to write a personal narrative focused on one's own unique individuality seems a relatively recent historical development.[2] In fact Paul Delaney, in his extremely helpful study of British autobiographies of the seventeenth century, argues that autobiography existed neither as a recognized genre nor even as a descriptive term during and preceding the Renaissance (1). Moreover, Delaney contends that autobiography *per se* was relatively rare in the middle ages—a fact he ascribes to that period's cultural insensitivity to historical change (8). With the Renaissance came a more relativistic sense of history and a greater awareness of the past; these factors, combined with wider and deeper literacy and a growing concern with genealogy, prompted more and more people to write about their families' pasts in ways that led to an emphasis on their own existence in the present (Delaney 8–9). Moulsworth's poem exhibits many of these characteristics, especially in its emphasis on the lineage of her father and third husband and in its implied and explicit evidence of the learning both she and her father enjoyed. Moulsworth seems as proud of her father's genteel descent and Oxford degree as of her third husband's coat of arms, and in both respects her poem illustrates Delaney's claims associating the rise of autobiography with family pride and the spread of literacy within the upper classes.[3] The personal interest in education that Moulsworth's father nurtured at Oxford was one he passed on to his daughter.

Delaney also claims that another factor promoting the rise of autobiography during the Renaissance was an increasing capacity for people to imagine themselves playing different social roles in response to changing circumstances or evolving personal beliefs. Particularly in the aftermath of the Reformation, the period exhibited a high degree of religious contention, social mobility, personal soul-searching, and individual insecurity (Delaney 11–15; 19–21). Although Moulsworth's poem gives little hint of any doctrinal uncertainty or any crises in her personal faith, she nevertheless had been thrice married and thrice widowed, and thus knew how greatly a person's sense of self could be affected by external circumstances. She claims, of course, that her husbands were "all louely, lovinge all," but then she immediately modifies the claim by adding the phrase "some more, some lesse" (l. 47). In this way she seems to acknowledge what must obviously have been true: that being a wife to three different husbands at three different periods in her own life would have made her acutely aware of the impact of both change and chance on one's personal history.

Delaney claims that autobiographical writing in the seventeenth century was often a response to the shock of some other external stimuli (38), and certainly the repeated deaths of Moulsworth's children and husbands, and especially her most recent widowhood, may have contributed to her impulse to write.[4] Her repeated periods of isolation would have sharpened her sense of herself as a unique individual, especially since each experience of living alone, like each experience of marriage, would have been subtly or even significantly different from the others. More than many people, Moulsworth would have had opportunities to ponder both her relations with others and her own sense of self. Of course, as a woman she must have felt the impact of social relations all the more acutely, and her autobiography is largely the story of her dealings with the different males whose presences and absences so strongly affected her life.[5] From those dealings, however, Moulsworth seems also to have developed a strong sense of her own personality, so that she concludes her life history by vowing to marry no more.

Delaney argues that the writing of autobiography requires an author's awareness of personal significance, and he contends that such awareness was often rooted in strong religious belief, which taught the equal dignity of all souls (18). Many autobiographies seem to have grown out of the habit of keeping religious diaries (Delaney 63), and certainly Moulsworth's poem seems rooted in her basic confidence that she mattered not only to her father and husbands but especially to her God.[6] Yet her work displays little of the tortured self-consciousness that Delaney finds typical of many Calvinist autobiographies of the period, whose authors often depicted themselves "cowering before a wrathful God" (60). Instead, her poem seems to reflect a sense of self-respect probably implanted by her father, but one that may also have been typical of more and more women of her time. Her impulse to write an autobiography may thus tell us something about changes that were taking place not only in the larger culture (with its growing emphasis on individual identity) but also in the minds of Renaissance women in particular.

When Moulsworth finally sat down to write her "Memorandum," she would have had precious few models to follow. Since the genre of autobiography was so recent that it had not yet even been named, individual authors were not only free, but to some extent were also forced, to invent their own approaches to their task. This fact makes Moulsworth's role as a pioneering autobiographer all the more significant, but in some ways it must also have made her project even more daunting. As Delaney points out, a philosophical justification for writing about one's private, secular experiences had not yet fully developed (107), and indeed Moulsworth's poem can be viewed as one of the earliest products of a growing trend toward seeing some value in recording the details of individual lives. Writing about oneself was still considered somewhat disreputable by many persons (Delaney 16), and this fact may help account for Moulsworth's heavy emphasis on her relations with others, particularly with important males (including God). Men who chose to write about themselves could always keep their focus on their public deeds, social accomplishments, or interesting travels, or they could emphasize the larger social or historical events in which they had been involved (Delaney 16).[7] Moulsworth's focus was necessarily more private, yet she largely avoids the apologetic tone that accompanies so many of the period's efforts to set out the details of individual lives (Delaney 108). Instead, she seems to take the value of her story largely for granted, and she seems untroubled by many of the inhibitions which, according to Delaney, inhibited the free self-expression of other Renaissance autobiographers (108). Perhaps because she did not intend her work for publication or wide circulation, she seems not to have worried excessively about the potential reactions of her readers. In any event, the most controversial aspects of her poem tend to be brief, mild, and good-humored.

Of course, Moulsworth's tone of polished, civilized restraint may have as much to do with her economic class, religious affiliation, and social circumstances as with her innate "personality." Presumably she was an Anglican, and according to Delaney, autobiographies written by members of the established church tended to be more genteel than those composed by members of dissenting sects (18). Anglican works were much less likely to engage in intimate self-revelation, and since Anglican priests were "usually gentlemen's sons and also in a sense 'gentry' among ministers of religion, [they] tended to write with measured, objective soberness"

(Delaney 18). The same adjectives and noun might just as easily fit the poem by Moulsworth, who was herself, of course, the daughter of an Anglican minister who happened to belong to the gentry. Paradoxically, had Moulsworth been a member of a dissenting sect, her poem might have been much more conventional than it is: dissenters often followed well-worn patterns, since their works were conceived not simply as personal narratives but as pieces of sectarian propaganda, designed to convert others as much as to explain a single life (Delaney 27). More conservative autobiographers, presumably including Moulsworth, tended to work more independently; their works were less frequently designed for publication, and Anglicans in particular tended to leave their writings in manuscript (Delaney 18).[8] Moulsworth seems to fit these patterns, and the fact that she was a woman would only have enhanced the likelihood that her narrative would be distinctive. Autobiographers in general had few generic models to follow; there were few classical or medieval precedents to imitate, and contemporary foreign influences were just barely felt (Delaney 7; 32; 109–11). If Moulsworth had been writing for publication or as a member of a dissenting religious sect, she would have been under greater pressure to conform to external expectations, not only about content but also about structure and style. Instead, her poem almost perfectly illustrates Delaney's claim that "seventeenth-century autobiography, in Britain at least, has a greater variety of individual forms than any other genre, and in fact drew on most other genres for inspiration, according to each autobiographer's social position and literary taste" (22–23). Moulsworth's "Memorandum," distinctive enough simply by being the work of a woman, seems additionally distinctive in view of its highly individual design.

The fact that autobiographical writing was still largely uncharted territory may have enhanced Moulsworth's sense of freedom, but it may also have heightened her need and desire to create a serious and well-crafted work. Precisely because she had no predetermined form to follow, she may have been all the more conscious of the need to impose a discernible structure on her poem. Had her work been more strictly religious in its emphasis, she might have been influenced more strongly by patterns suggested by the Psalms, the prophets, the book of Job, Pauline conversion narratives, Catholic mysticism, or Calvinist accounts of the spiritual struggle for inner assurance (see Delaney 28–36). However, her largely secular focus threw her back much more squarely on her own creative resources and thus contributed to her poem's originality. As Delaney contends, in the seventeenth century it was easier to write about one's relations with God than about relations with other people, because a strictly religious writer could look toward sermons for models or toward "a long tradition of devotional literature" (107). Conversely, secular autobiographies of the period reveal "a bewildering multiplicity of themes and literary forms, with each autobiographer groping for a means of self-expression suited to his particular needs" (Delaney 107). Moulsworth's poem would seem to illustrate this contention; the highly strucured and self-conscious design of her work may in fact reflect her sense of the need to impose a discernible form rather than to borrow a predetermined pattern.

Of course, the distinction between "secular" and "religious" autobiography is largely artificial, as Delaney readily admits and as Moulsworth's poem so clearly illustrates (107–08). In her case as in so many others, the difference is mainly a matter of emphasis. Moulsworth obviously wrote with God constantly in mind, but she devotes far less space to recounting her religious development than to tracing the history of her relations with other human beings. In this sense her poem exemplifies a number of Delaney's other contentions about "secular" autobiographers, such as the claim that while clergy generally wrote religious autobiographies, secular works were more often composed by lay persons (108). Moulsworth's poem also seems to fit another of Delaney's patterns, since he contends that secular autobiographies were more likely to be written by persons of higher social rank (122). It seems doubtful that if Moulsworth had been born the daughter of a peasant or if she had been the wife of three successive yeomen her poem would ever have been written—or at least not in its present form. The mere fact that it was composed as a highly sophisticated and self-consciously "literary" poem suggests something about its author's social identity and intellectual aspirations. Indeed, the "Memorandum" exemplifies many characteristics that Delaney ascribes to a group of secular autobiographers he calls "the Individualists":

> They were all respectable citizens, mostly from old families whose wealth was based on land. They observed deco-

rum and moderation in their manner of life and in the way they wrote about it ... [although] they were not writing for the general public. In religion they were Protestant with High Church leanings. Their judgements on human affairs tended to be made from a firmly moral, but not superstitiously providential point of view.... Indulging in neither the hysterical self-accusation of the extreme sectaries, nor the militant certainties of the Catholics, they preferred to follow a decent and pious middle way. Several of them had bookish inclinations, but none were professional scholars or authors; their literary styles are usually clear, unadorned, and correct, in contrast to [the writings of other, more] eccentric stylists.... Finally, though they were in some ways bourgeois in outlook they lacked the industrious acquisitiveness typical of Whig merchants and businessmen; they were generally born to wealth and did not show conspicuous energy in adding to it. They were more likely to retire and enjoy what they had in peace. (151)

Few passages from Delaney's study better sum up so many of the traits of Moulsworth's poem, although in her case it is always worth remembering how her status as a woman would have affected both her writing and her existence. As a woman, for instance, she would have been all the more concerned to display a "respectable" life, and she would have had little opportunity to acquire wealth through means other than inheritance or marriage. Her religious affiliation would have been as much a matter of her father's or husbands' influences as of her own free choice, and, even more than most men, she would have been expected to display a pious moral outlook. As a woman of intelligence, learning, and social status, she might have been all the more anxious to seem reasonable and free from hysterics, and for the same reason she may have wanted to show her mastery of a discourse that was both clear and correct (if not entirely unadorned).[9] Finally, her lack of any conspicuous involvement with worldly affairs would have been due as much to the accident of her sex as to the inherent nature of her character. Moulsworth may have written in a relatively "restrained" style because she seems to have been religiously conservative (see Delaney 32), but she may also have written that way because such a style would have been expected of someone of her class and gender. Her relative lack of egotism may have reflected an innate modesty, but it may also have been the kind of personality a woman was expected to display (see Delaney 126).[10]

It is, of course, as a *woman's* autobiography that Moulsworth's poem is especially intriguing. Studying the work from this perspective allows us to see the various ways in which the "Memorandum" relates not only to other autobiographical writings by early modern women, but also to more general theoretical claims about the nature of feminine autobiography. Delaney asserts, for instance, that early modern women lacked the "firm identification with profession or occupation which was typical of their male counterparts" (158), and certainly this seems true in Moulsworth's case. She was defined—and defines herself—not in terms of any job, but rather in terms of her social roles and her relations with important males. Like many of the other women autobiographers Delaney surveyed, Moulsworth does not adopt "a consistently and exclusively religious point of view," nor does she write "within any particular convention of religious autobiography" (158). Denied access to any formal religious training and barred from any employment in the church, Moulsworth wrote a kind of work typical of many other women from her period: one in which religion is surely a major emphasis but inevitably not a professional concern. "Perhaps as a result of this relatively weak vocational interest," Delaney claims,

> female autobiographers strike the modern reader as having, generally, a more "unified sensibility" than their male counterparts: their lives seem less compartmentalized, they have a wider range of emotional responses to everyday events and more awareness of concrete realities. (158)

In many ways this seems true of Moulsworth, whose poem seems to express a calm, equable approach to life, and whose tone can seem both feisty and contented, both opinionated and serene. Yet it always seems worth bearing in mind that Moulsworth's focus on "everyday events" and "concrete realities" resulted at least in part from the fact that her life *was* compartmentalized—that as a woman she was denied access to many of the kinds of experience that would have allowed her to be either more speculative and abstract or more full of worldly ambition.[11] Like many other women autobiographers, she does indeed seem "more concerned" with expressing "intimate feelings" than with recording public acts (see Delaney 159), but it should never be forgotten that this focus was partly a forced choice dictated by her gender.

Like the handful of female autobiographers Delaney discusses, Moulsworth came from a genteel background (159), and she also shares with those women a penchant for formal idiosyncrasy: "they freely adapted conventional narrative modes to suit their individual tastes and preoccupations" (Delaney 165). Yet Moulsworth also stands apart from Delaney's group in significant respects, since all the members of that group "wrote their lives after the Restoration," and since "all were born between 1620 and 1625" (159). Of course, the fact that Moulsworth lived and wrote so much earlier only enhances the interest of her poem and makes its historical significance all the more obvious. In fact, her work is even more intriguing because of its highly personal focus; many of the earliest autobiographical writings by women in the seventeenth century, such as the activist political tracts that emerged during the Civil War, tend to be conventional in design, didactic in purpose, and relatively impersonal in their tones and concerns (Graham 2–3). Often resembling religious conversion narratives, these works tended to be made public only after the intervention of male editors and only if they conformed to predetermined doctrinal expectations: "Only those that could be interpreted as proper models would find publication in this way" (Graham 4; 20). Moulsworth's poem, in contrast, seems much more personal in both its genesis, its textual history, and its form; the mere fact that it was written in verse, for instance, makes it already unusual among the other autobiographical writings of women from the first half of the seventeenth century (Graham 4–6).[12]

On the other hand, Moulsworth's poem shares a number of features with other autobiographies from her time. Many of those works, for example, discuss the experience of some kinds of oppression, including those associated with marriage (Graham 23), and certainly Moulsworth's sardonic comments about the marriage market and her vigorous protest against unequal education fit this pattern. Yet her poem also illustrates the immediately subsequent claim that "It would be wrong ... to imply that the female perspective is a consistently gloomy one; the defiance and delights of these women are expressed in both small and large ways" (Graham 23). Certainly this is true of the "Memorandum," which manages to convey a good deal of satisfaction about a life that nevertheless involved real and repeated pain. In addition, Moulsworth's poem exhibits another major trait associated with other female autobiographers from her century: "a high level of awareness of the actual writing process" (Graham 23). In Moulsworth's case this self-consciousness is particularly evident, perhaps in part because Moulsworth was attempting a kind of writing for which there was very little precedent. Indeed, the fact that she really was attempting something fairly new may help to account for another feature her poem shares with many of the female autobiographies that followed it: a reliance on Biblical phrasing. Since Moulsworth and similar writers would be read by "a public of bible-owners and readers," scriptural language would serve "to make their narratives more accessible, as well as giving a broader meaning to their activities" (Graham 23; 6). By adopting the central discourse of their Christian culture, women autobiographers could give their works a kind of sanction they might otherwise lack. They could express their own sincere opinions while also disarming potential critics. In fact a concern with reputation and self-defense often seems to have been a motive for many autobiographies by women in the seventeenth century (Graham 24), although Moulsworth's focus, on the whole, seems more introspective and meditative than confrontational and combative. Thus, despite the fact that she overtly champions women's rights, her tone rarely seems strident or defensive. Although Moulsworth seems to have been less concerned than some other women writers with defending or defining her personal reputation (Graham 24), she does seem to share their basic desire "to make the truth about themselves known" (Graham 16). Even this desire, of course, could be construed as a way of protesting (or at least circumventing) the silence ordinarily imposed on their sex. Even the mere act of writing one's life could be seen as an assertion of social identity and personal dignity.

Recent feminist critics have claimed, in fact, that especially for a woman of Moulsworth's era, the mere desire to write one's life could represent a transgression against "patriarchal definitions of female nature"; yet such transgression, paradoxically, often involved "enacting the scenario of male selfhood" (Sidonie Smith, *A Poetics* 8). In other words, a woman might violate certain cultural stereotypes or inherited values by seeking to write, but she might also reinforce related stereotypes and values by writing in a style or in forms associated with the dominant culture. Sidonie Smith notes, in fact, that according to certain French feminists, "women's true autobiography has yet to be written, since women writers have, until recently, only reinscribed male writing and thereby produced a text 'which either obscures women or reproduces the classic representations of women'" (*A Poetics* 18). According to one feminist whom Smith quotes, this predicament presents for any potential woman autobiographer a "double bind: 'As long as women remain silent, they will be outside the historical process. But, if they begin to speak and write *as men do*, they will enter history subdued and alienated'" (*A Poetics* 18). It is certainly possible to read Moulsworth's poem as a symptom of this double bind: despite her explicit protests against the cultural restrictions placed on women, her own poem can be seen as strongly patriarchal, both in the Christian worldview it ultimately endorses and in its highly structured, carefully wrought style. Of course, to read the poem this way is not to blame Moulsworth for failing to be completely "liberated"—a charge both somewhat silly and clearly anachronistic. Rather, reading the poem as almost a patriarchal document in spite of itself would simply mean acknowledging the extremely complicated cultural position in which a woman writer such as Moulsworth inevitably was placed. Obviously she yearns for a greater measure of female autonomy, yet ultimately she does, in some sense, reinscribe many of the most basic cultural and aesthetic values of a society dominated by men.

Some French feminists contend, in fact, that the very act of writing autobiography "is ultimately an assertion of arrival and embeddedness in the phallic order" (Sidonie Smith, *A Poetics*, 40). This claim helps makes sense, for instance, of Moulsworth's strong emphasis on the familial heritage of her father and third husband, since the "myth of origins reenacted in the pages of the autobiographical text asserts the primacy of patrilineal descent and, with it, androcentric discourse" (Sidonie Smith, *A Poetics* 40). In addition, such a claim may also help to explain Moulsworth's total silence concerning her mother, since the autobiographer "must erase the matrilineal trace by suppressing the name of the mother and all female subjectivity unmediated by

male representation" (Sidonie Smith, *A Poetics* 40). Thus the
women whom Moulsworth extols in her poem are either the fanci-
ful, fictive muses or the Biblical Mary, who ignored stereoptypi-
cal "women's work" to sit at the feet of Jesus and imbibe his word.
Indeed, Moulsworth vows to transmute the faulty model provided
by the Biblical Martha, the archetypal busy housewife: Mouls-
worth plans to "dight" (or make ready) her "Inward house" (l.
19) and thus prepare an appropriate habitation for Christ. In so
doing, it could be argued, Moulsworth accepts the symbolic deni-
gration of women's work and "silences that part of herself that
identifies her as a daughter of her mother. Repressing the
mother in her, she turns away from the locus of all that is domes-
ticated and disempowered culturally and erases the trace of sex-
ual difference and desire" (Sidonie Smith, *A Poetics* 53). Even
Moulsworth's constant citations of scripture can be seen as at-
tempts to make her own words replicate the Word—the domi-
nant, authorizing male speech of her culture. Moulsworth might
thus seem to fit the pattern of the female autobiographer de-
scribed by Sidonie Smith. According to Smith, such a writer

> "raises herself," as Julia Kristeva argues, "to the symbolic
> stature of her father." Identifying with the father and his
> law, she opts for the scenario of public achievement that
> apparently structures traditional autobiography and
> grounds the authority to write about herself in the fit of
> her life to stories of the representative man. To the extent
> that she reinscribes the myth of origins embedded in the
> discourse of man, she justifies her claim to membership in
> the world of words, men, and public spaces, adapting and
> thereby reproducing the myth of paternal origins and the
> narratives it underwrites. (*A Poetics* 52–53)

According to this view, Smith says, "the autobiographer who
speaks like a man becomes essentially a 'phallic woman,' an arti-
ficial or man-made product turned in the cultural and linguistic
machinery of androcentric discourse" (*A Poetics* 53). Moulsworth's
radical proposal to found a women's university can be seen, from
this perspective, as both a capitulation to, and a recapitulation
of, "the symbolic order of patriarchy" (Sidonie Smith, *A Poetics*
53). By issuing her proposal and even by writing her poem (it
might be argued), Moulsworth not only seeks "the cultural recog-

nition that flows to her as a person who embodies male-identi-
fied ideals; but she also [thereby] perpetuates the political, so-
cial, and textual disempowerment of mothers and daughters"
(Sidonie Smith, *A Poetics* 53). The fact that Moulsworth's poem
is so consciously and carefully crafted and so focused on describing
her relations with men can easily be seen as evidence that even
the most assertive women writers of her time were inevitably
coopted by the larger patriarchal culture. This cooptation was a
kind of containment, it might be said, from which women could
never quite break free, partly because their culture made it virtu-
ally impossible for them even to imagine what such freedom
might entail. Moulsworth's poem, it might be claimed, provides
stunning evidence of how even a highly intelligent and thought-
ful woman of that era could not help but remain, ultimately, a du-
tiful daughter and wife.

The factors contributing to this kind of alleged containment
are not far to seek. Sidonie Smith contends, for instance, that the
"meaning culture assigns to sexual difference, that is, the ideol-
ogy of gender, has always constituted *a*, if not *the*, fundamental
ideological system for interpreting and understanding individual
identity and social dynamics" (*A Poetics* 48). And, since
"traditional autobiography has functioned as one of those forms
and languages that sustain sexual difference, the woman who
writes autobiography is doubly estranged when she enters the au-
tobiographical contract" (Sidonie Smith, *A Poetics* 49). In fact,
Smith quotes and then comments on Nancy K. Miller's claim that
"'female autobiographers know that they are being read as
women.' They understand that a statement or a story will receive
a different ideological interpretation if attributed to a man or to
a woman" (*A Poetics* 49). For this reason, the imagined or pro-
jected (male) reader exerts even more influence over the feminine
autobiographer than is generally true in the case of other au-
thors. In Smith's formulation, "The one who remains silent and
who listens exerts power over the one who speaks" (*A Poetics* 49).
The extreme degree of self-consciousness implied by this assess-
ment might help to explain Moulsworth's obvious preoccupation
with formal patterning and rhetorical sophistication; whether
deliberately or not, she may have designed her poem to forestall
the criticism of literate readers, and particularly of educated
males. In this respect Moulsworth's poem may illustrate a gen-

eral claim Smith makes about the feminine autobiographer: "Acutely sensitive to her reader's expectations and to her own often conflicting desires, she negotiates a sometimes elegant, sometimes cramped balance of anticipated reader expectations and responsive authorial maneuvers" (*A Poetics* 50). For instance, Moulsworth's strong religious emphasis undoubtedly reflects "her own" beliefs, but it may also reflect her recognition that "she can speak with authority only insofar as she tells a story that her audience will read" (Smith, *A Poetics* 52).

This emphasis on the influence of an imagined or implied audience goes hand in hand with an emphasis on Moulsworth as a woman, highly influenced by her status in a patriarchal culture. In fact, it could be argued that her status as a woman made Moulsworth herself already a kind of text; the allowable meanings and permitted limits of her life were already, in this sense, dictated or pre-scribed. Writing her autobiography could in one sense be a way for her to attempt to impose some measure of personal control over the significance of her existence, but such control could inevitably be only partial and incomplete. Of course, it might be claimed that the same is true of any member of any culture, but strong cultural influence is likely to be particularly strongly felt by women or the members of other "marginal" groups. Such groups, it can be claimed, inevitably live less autonomous lives and can thus only produce less autonomous writings. Indeed, more than many other genres, autobiography raises most strikingly the whole question of who or what an author is— of who or what inscribes or "authorizes" a text.

Moulsworth, for instance, obviously worked hard to impose a highly finished order and coherence on her "Memorandum," and in some senses she clearly achieved the kind of aesthetic balance and personal integration highlighted in the first chapter of this study. Yet her text can also be seen as far less stable, far less finally coherent and harmonious than that chapter suggests. Particularly when viewed as a piece of autobiographical writing, and especially when viewed as a woman's attempt to inscribe her own life, the "Memorandum" can be viewed in quite problematic terms. Rather than being seen as an achievement of coherent aesthetic harmony, it can instead be viewed as a site of ideological contention—a battleground populated by inconsistent impulses, conflicting vocabularies, discordant discourses, and incompatible ideals. Viewed from this kind of perspective, the "Memorandum" becomes a work requiring what Barbara Johnson has called "'the careful teasing out of warring forces of signification within the text itself'" (qtd. in Sidonie Smith, *A Poetics* 6). Moulsworth's simultaneous "feminist" protest and Christian deference, for instance, would be only the most obvious examples of such contending voices.[13]

A full feminist reading of the "Memorandum" will be offered in the following chapter; for the present it simply seems worth noting how fully Moulsworth's poem implies the kinds of questions central to recent theorizing about the difficulties and paradoxes inherent in any attempt to write one's life, particularly when the life in question is a woman's. Shari Benstock argues, for instance, that "autobiography reveals the impossibility of its own dream: what begins on the presumption of self-knowledge ends in the creation of a fiction that covers over the premises of its construction" (11). According to Benstock, in traditional theories of autobiography,

> the fabric of the [autobiographical] narrative appears seamless, spun of whole cloth. The effect is magical—the self apears organic, the present the sum total of the past, the past an accurate predictor of the future. This conception of the autobiographical rests on a firm belief in the *conscious* control of artist over subject matter; this view of the life history is grounded in authority. (19)

Benstock and others allege that this patriarchal view of autobiography privileges narratives emphasizing synthesis and harmony, and indeed some critics have stressed that traditional notions of autobiography are inevitably rooted in a male-centered view of the isolated, autonomous self. However, according to Susan Stanford Friedman, this "emphasis on individualism does not take into account the importance of a culturally imposed group identity for women and minorities" (34). In other words, "individualistic paradigms of the self ignore the role of collective and relational identities in the individuation process of women and minorities" (Friedman 35). In fact, the emphasis on the unique individual in traditional theories of autobiography can itself be seen as a product of the philosophy of individualism that became increasingly important in Western culture during and after the Renaissance (Friedman 34). Indeed, in this sense Moulsworth's poem can be seen as both a reflection of and response to the rise of this growing emphasis on the unique significance of individual lives. Moulsworth might thus be seen as participating in a subtle revolution of thought, especially in her insistence on women's rights to equal education. At the same time, however, her poem can also be seen as reflecting the degree to which any woman's life was inevitably far from autonomous—that is, the extent to which individual women were far from being treated or defined (even by themselves) simply as individuals. Moulsworth's poem supports the arguments of those critics (like Friedman) who stress instead the impact (for good or ill) of communal values and social relations on the lives and writings of women (38). For this reason, "the self constructed in women's autobiographical writing is often based in, but not limited to, a group consciousness—an awareness of the meaning of the cultural category WOMAN for the patterns of women's individual destiny" (Friedman 40–41).

Friedman's argument, in fact, can help account for both the genesis and the specific features of a poem like Moulsworth's. Friedman suggests that because women often recognize the disparities between cultural stereotypes and their own lived experience, they can often "develop a dual consciousness—the self as culturally defined and the self as different from cultural prescription" (39). Indeed, in many cases (perhaps including Moulsworth's), such "alienation from the historically imposed image of the self is what motivates the writing, the creation of an alternate self in the autobiographical act" (Friedman 41). The kind of duality that Friedman stresses can be glimpsed, for instance, in Moulsworth's simultaneous protest and deference—in the clear hostility to some forms of male dominance that nonetheless exists side by side with an equally clear affection for many individual men.[14] Citing the work of Nancy Chodorow, which emphasizes a "relational model of female selfhood," Friedman argues that "we can anticipate finding in women's texts a consciousness of self in which 'the individual does not oppose herself to all others,' nor 'feel herself to exist outside of others,' 'but very much *with* others in an interdependent existence'" (41). In fact, this emphasis on relatedness and interdependence can be seen even in Friedman's own scholarship, since she cites Mary Mason citing Simone de

Beauvoir's argument that "men have cast women into the role of 'the other' existing only in relation to the male identity," whereas Mason contends that women often "seem to recognize the full autonomy of the 'other' (in this case the male) without destroying their own sense of self" (Friedman 43). Such a view of the woman autobiographer's poise and equanimity may in fact help explain the "balance" that so strongly characterizes Moulsworth's poem. Moulsworth, it might be argued, had spent her entire life engaged in a subtle balancing act. From girlhood on, she had had to accommodate her own sense of self to the expectations imposed upon her as a woman. The command she exhibits over so many aspects of her poem may therefore simply reflect a self-command and self-possession that she had developed partly in response to the circumstances imposed by her gender.

In fact, Mary Mason herself argues that women who write about their lives have shown no interest in replicating the standard narrative patterns set down by men. "Nowhere in women's autobiographies," she asserts, "do we find the patterns established by the two prototypical male autobiogaphers, Augustine and Rousseau" (21). By the same token, she contends, "male writers never take up the archetypal models" of female autobiography her essay examines (Mason 21). Women, she claims, ignore the "structure of conversion" emphasized by Augustine's *Confessions,* "where the self is presented as a stage for a battle of opposing forces and where a climactic victory for one force—spirit defeating flesh—completes the drama of the self." This structure "simply does not accord with the deepest realities of women's experience and so is inappropriate as a model for women's life writing" (Mason 22). By the same token, Rousseau's model, which emphasizes "an unfolding self-discovery where characters and events are little more than aspects of the author's evolving consciousness, finds no echo in women's writing about their lives" (Mason 22). Instead, Mason insists (and Moulsworth's poem would in fact seem to illustrate) that

> the self-discovery of female identity seems to acknowledge the real presence and recognition of another consciousness, and the disclosure of female self is linked to the identification of some 'other.' This recognition of another consciousness—and I emphasize recognition of rather than deference to—this grounding of identity through relation to the cho-

sen other, seems ... to enable women to write openly about themselves. (22)

Of course, the strongly categorical nature of Mason's assertions renders them questionable: conversion narratives, for instance, were among the most popular forms for women autobiographers in the seventeenth century (Graham 3–4), and it has been claimed that Mason's "suggestion that women's autobiographies are typified by presentations of the self defined in relations to others depends on an implausible idea that men's do not, or implies that women have a more reactive and consciously relational sense of self than men" (Graham 21). Nonetheless, although Mason's claims are far too sweeping to apply without exception, in important respects they do seem to fit Moulsworth's "Memorandum." Moulsworth's poem does exhibit little emphasis on conversion, little emphasis on an egoistic, evolving self, but it does display great emphasis on relations with others and specifically with important men.[15] Moulsworth seems to have been able, in life as in her poem, to acknowledge the influence of these men without surrendering to it completely. Indeed, one of the paradoxes of both her poem and her life is that the self-confidence that seems to have permitted her to write at all was nurtured by her relations with such significant males as her father, her third husband, and God. In her attitudes toward these figures, as in the structure and meanings of her poem, she seems to have been able to attain a careful poise and equilibrium, a finely wrought balance. It is this kind of aesthetic and experiential complexity that lends an enduring interest both to the life she lived and to the life she wrote. Her poem, fascinating simply as the record of an individual life, is equally intriguing as one of our culture's first autobiographies by a woman.

Notes

1. Sara Mendelson notes that, in "their literary form, journals and memoirs varied as much as the women who composed them. Seventeenth-century memoirs had not yet crystallized into their modern-day forms, the diary and the autobiography." See

"Stuart Women's Diaries," 181–82. Also helpful on this topic is an essay by Betty Travitsky, "'His Wife's Prayers and Meditations': MS Egerton 607," in *The Renaissance Englishwoman in Print*, ed. Anne M. Haselkorn and Betty S. Travitsky, 241–62. Also valuable is an essay by Mary Beth Rose: "Gender, Genre, and History: Seventeenth-Century English Women and the Art of Autobiography," in *Women in the Middle Ages and the Renaissance: Literary and Historical Perspectives*, ed. Mary Beth Rose (Syracuse: Syracuse University Press, 1986), 245–78. However, Rose focuses mainly on four women who wrote in the latter half of the century. James M. Osborn briefly discusses an early Tudor autobiography, by a male writer, in *The Beginnings of Autobiography in England* (Los Angeles: William Andrews Clark Memorial Library, 1959). See also Margaret Bottrall, *Every Man a Phoenix: Studies in Seventeenth-Century Autobiography* (London: John Murray, 1958), esp. 10–11. On the genre generally, see the helpful bibliographical essay appended to William C. Spengemann's *The Forms of Autobiography: Episodes in the History of a Literary Genre* (New Haven and London: Yale University Press, 1980).

Works which have proven exceptionally helpful in writing this chapter include the following: Shari Benstock, ed., *The Private Self: Theory and Practice of Women's Autobiographical Writings* (Chapel Hill and London: University of North Carolina Press, 1988); Paul Delaney, *British Autobiography in the Seventeenth Century* (New York: Columbia University Press, 1969); Susan Stanford Friedman, "Women's Autobiographical Selves: Theory and Practice," in *The Private Self*, edited by Shari Benstock, 34–62. Elspeth Graham, Hillary Hinds, Elaine Hobby, and Helen Wilcox, eds., *Her Own Life: Autobiographical Writings by Seventeenth-Century Englishwomen* (London and New York: Routledge, 1989); Mary G. Mason, "The Other Voice: Autobiographies of Women Writers," in *Life / Lines: Theorizing Women's Autobiography*, edited by Bella Broadzki and Celeste Schenck (Ithaca and London: Cornell University Press, 1988), 19–44; James Olney, *Metaphors of Self: The Meaning of Autobiography* (Princeton: Princeton University Press, 1972); and Sidonie Smith, *A Poetics of Women's Autobiography: Marginality and the Fictions of Self-Representation* (Bloomington and Indianapolis: Indiana University Press, 1987).

2. Elizabeth W. Bruss cautions that we tend to "read older texts, or texts of other cultures, and find in them autobiographical intentions, but it is often our own conventions which inform this reading and give the text this force." See *Autobiographical Acts: The Changing Situation of a Literary Genre* (Baltimore and London: Johns Hopkins University Press, 1976), 6.

3. Sara Mendelson notes that a "major disadvantage" of the material she considers "is that it is not representative of women as a whole but only that élite minority who had learned to write. One undisputed attribute of the seventeenth-century female population is its overwhelming illiteracy with respect to writing skills.... No example has survived of a female diary below the level of the middle class." See "Stuart Women's Diaries," 182–83. Helen Wilcox also comments on the effects of class on feminine autobiography; see "Private Writing and Public Function," 48.

4. On a related point, see Janet Varner Gunn, *Autobiography: Toward a Poetics of Experience* (Philadelphia: University of Pennsylvania Press, 1982), 16.

5. Interestingly, the only other women Moulsworth mentions are either mythical (the muses) or Biblical. She shows little interest in discussing her friendships (if any) with other women, not even female relatives. Linda Woodbridge discusses male distrust of friendships among women in *Women and the English Renaissance*, 237.

6. In her article on "Stuart Women's Diaries," Sara Mendelson notes that "three-quarters of the works in the present sample contain considerable devotional content.... Of course, to some extent this profusion of devotional literature reflects the real importance of religion in the lives of seventeenth-century women. Indeed, the female sex was thought to exceed the male in that particular virtue" (185).

7. On this point see also Sara Mendelson, "Stuart Women's Diaries," 199.

8. The four autobiographers whom Mary Beth Rose studies were also traditional upper-class Anglicans. Rose notes that, viewed "from historical perspective, the traditionalism of these women—their attachment to established patriarchal values and goals—can be seen to have played a paradoxical role in freeing them to write." See her essay "Gender, Genre, and History," 273.

9. Linda Woodbridge notes that male Renaissance writers often associated female speech with "meaningless sound, babbling, prating, chattering"; see *Women and the English Renaissance,* 210.

10. Angeline Goreau notes the "inhibitions" placed on women's ways of "speaking, looking, walking, imagining, thinking." She also claims that the "reinterpretation of 'chastity' as a figurative rather than literal inhibition created an infinitely expanding architecture of self-restraint—often more far-reaching and effective than any form of external censorship might be." See *The Whole Duty of a Woman,* 10; 13.

11. On this point, see Sara Mendelson, "Stuart Women's Diaries," 195.

12. On the "unpolished mode" of much autobiographical writing by women during this period, see Helen Wilcox, "Private Writing and Public Function," 49.

13. Shirley Neuman calls for a "poetics of differences [that] can mark autobiographical subjects' differences from other identities and from and within their own identities. It can also mark the nodes of intersubjectivity that occur as the autobiographical 'I' is 'called momentarily' into this or that discourse, this or that subject-position." See her essay "Autobiography: From Different Poetics to a Poetics of Differences," 226.

14. Similarly, it has recently been claimed that the "autobiographical occasion (whether performance or text) becomes a site on which cultural ideologies intersect and dissect one another, in contradiction, consonance, and adjacency. Thus the site is rife with diverse potentials...." See the "Introduction" to *De/colonizing the Subject: The Politics of Gender in Women's Autobiography,* ed. Sidonie Smith and Julia Watson (Minneapolis: University of Minnesota Press, 1992), xix.

15. Similarly, Helen Wilcox notes, concerning the subjects of her essay, that despite "their separateness of function, the husband in the 'world' and the wife in the 'house,' these women often found their lives, and hence their texts, structured around their husbands." See "Private Writing and Public Function," 50.

Chapter 4

FEMINIST CONTEXTS

Positioning Moulsworth's "Memorandum" in feminist criticism would require multiple readings or approaches, since feminist theory is not a single approach but many. Yet as Annette Kolodny points out, the pluralism or diversity associated with feminist criticism is part of its strength, even though conflicts and contradictions are inevitable.[1] Since multiple readings are possible and entirely appropriate, Moulsworth's poem can be examined in light of several critical approaches. Some are politically and socially based (as seen in the predominantly American responses) and others are psychoanalytically, philosophically, and linguistically based (as in the French theories), but all the approaches come under the rubric of feminist criticism. Generally the Anglo-American critics work within the existing political system and seek equality. In literature this approach means accepting established definitions of what constitutes literature. The French feminists resist working within existing social and historical traditions and question the idea of literature itself. Their concern is with female creativity that is unfiltered through patriarchal concepts of literature and, in a somewhat utopian vision, untainted by patriarchal language itself.[2] Employing a variety of approaches to examine Moulsworth's "Memorandum" exposes some of the artistic richness of the poem and at the same time highlights its historical importance. Thus the poem can be seen as part of a tradition of literature written by women who are linked across generations by common subjects and themes. For this reason the poem contributes to an understanding of female experience. At the same time, however, the poem can be analyzed as a text written by a woman who uses a language that, since it is part of the patriarchal culture, is alien to her. Studying the poem, then, can reveal a subversion of that culture.

One of the concerns of Anglo-American critics has been the establishment of a female literary tradition as a counterpart to the male literary tradition that one finds in the traditional canon.[3] In this approach, forgotten or lost works are retrieved and literature by women is examined for threads of commonality and connection. Discussing the importance of a female literary tradition, Virginia Woolf, in *A Room of One's Own*, argues that female writers build on the ground-breaking works of their literary ancestors or predecessors, since "masterpieces are not single and solitary births," and just as Marlowe needed Chaucer so did Jane Austen need Fanny Burney and all women writers needed Aphra Benn, "for it was she who earned them the right to speak their minds."[4] These literary ancestors have bequeathed to their heirs the right to write. Without forerunners, each writer has to demand the right anew and do so without the knowledge that cultural production is possible. Precisely because so much of women's contribution to literature has been erased, Elaine Showalter argues that "each generation of women writers has found itself, in a sense, without a history, forced to rediscover the past anew."[5] The discovery of lost writers ("spade work" criticism) not only brings to light previously unknown works but also provides models for aspiring writers, the importance of which is such that Alice Walker can write that "the life we save is our own."[6] Moulsworth's poem, though she did not seek publication, was clearly written for posterity, for an audience. In naming herself ("My Name was Martha"; l. 17), she uses the past tense, suggesting that the work will survive her, thus leaving a record of a woman's life, and that record will speak to others who struggle for a voice in a patriarchal culture, especially those who, after years of satisfying the demands of family, desire to write. In being discovered, the poem contributes to the female literary tradition, from which all women writers draw support.

Unfortunately, women often write in isolation. Women—as Ellen Moers contends in her study of nineteenth-century writers—were for the most part not in universities, were restricted in travel, and were essentially denied a public life.[7] It was not until the mid-nineteenth century that women were gaining acceptance as writers and were being allowed a public voice. However, their acceptance was still somewhat problematical, as Nathaniel Hawthorne's remark in 1854 about "that damned mob of scribbling women" illustrates.[8] For literary women, discussion or communication with like-minded peers often only took place through their fiction. They would draw on the works of other women writers for support or encouragement that was not forthcoming from other sources. Thus women writers often pay homage to other women: Emily Dickinson to Elizabeth Barrett Browning, for instance, and Browning to George Sand.[9] Even so, Browning lamented the absence of appropriate role models: "England has had many learned women ... and yet where are the poetesses?... I look everywhere for grandmothers, and see none."[10] Poetry, unlike novel writing (even after classical patterns were dropped), was often seen as somehow inappropriate for women. As Dickinson writes, "They shut me up in prose—" (*Poems*, #613). Moulsworth—in an age when personal journals, diaries, and letters were essentially the only acceptable forms for women—was even more isolated than her literary latter-day sisters. If her "Memorandum" can be taken as evidence, her role models were Biblical figures and her literary predecessors were the muses: "... the muses ffemalls are / and therefore of Vs ffemales take some care" (ll. 31–32).

Establishing a female literary tradition includes the uncovering of common threads in literature by women from one time period to another. Women, as Showalter in *A Literature of Their Own* suggests, react to cultural pressures and patriarchal institutions and incorporate "certain patterns, themes, problems, and images" in their texts (11). Consequently, "Women have had a literature of their own all along" (10). Thus while conditions varied from century to century, women's marginality persisted, creating a subculture or, to use an anthropological term, a muted group, and therefore similarities exist in women's responses to oppression and repression. Although Showalter focuses on nineteenth- and twentieth-century literature, common patterns can be traced through all time periods. Thus Moulsworth in the seventeenth century laments the lack of education for women, as do Maria Edgeworth in the eighteenth century (in *Letters to Literary Ladies*), Browning in the nineteenth century (in *Aurora Leigh*), and Woolf again in the twentieth century.

In addition to the discovery of common threads, the establishment of a female literary tradition would also make available the full range of female experiences which have been absent in the traditional canon, which contains, as Viviane Forrester contends, only what "men's eyes see."[11] Such an abnormality distorts perception; it leaves a vacuum and (in Forrester's words) "prohibits any global vision of the world, any vision of the human species" (181). Forrester calls for a "women's vision" (181) to provide a full and complete picture of humanity. Thus Moulsworth's discussion of her married life and her indication of her sexuality become significant. She adds a woman's perspective to complement the predominantly male one presented in the texts of the seventeenth century. Both sexes gain from an undistorted vision; no longer need women be the "dark continent."

Building a female literary tradition results in recovering forgotten writers and their works, but many women have in fact been silenced before ever putting pen to paper. While women appear frequently in literary works written by men as signs, constructs, symbols, or images, much more rarely have women been the producers of literary works. Virginia Woolf, in *A Room of One's Own*, recounts how a hypothetical sister of Shakespeare would have been silenced. Woolf imagines that Judith Shakespeare— denied an education, betrothed at a young age, and forbidden access to the stage—would have run away and been seduced and would then have committed suicide, never having written the plays of which she, like her brother, was capable (48–50). Woolf speculates on the effect that thwarting one's creativity has, and she suggests that whenever we hear of a madwoman or witch, "we are on the track of a lost novelist, a suppressed poet" (51). Likewise, Alice Walker speaks of "the agony of the lives of women who might have been Poets, Novelists, Essayists, and Short-Story Writers ... who died with their real gifts stifled within them."[12] Moulsworth avoided the fate of the madwoman or witch perhaps because she had the encouragment of her father, who provided her with an education unusual for girls, and perhaps because she had the magnanimity of her husbands, especially the third, who allowed her some control and independence: "I had my will in house, in purse in Store" (l. 67). Thus she found outlets for her intelligence. But with her "Memorandum" as an example of her potential, what might the possibilities have been if she had been given the same opportunities as a Sir Walter Ralegh or a John Donne?

A lack of education has been a serious obstacle for women desiring to write. Early in the eighteenth century, Alexander Pope voiced, in his "Essay on Criticism," the commonly-held view about the importance of a classical education: "Learn hence for ancient rules a just esteem; / To copy nature is to copy them."[13] Women denied such an education did not have the tools necessary to write serious poetry, which was traditionally based on Latin and Greek models. Women, therefore, were more apt to be part of the ballad tradition.[14] Moulsworth's early Latin training already made her an exception, but her strong criticism of the lack of education afforded women and her suggestion for creating a university for women made her even more exceptional. As late as the nineteenth century the argument was accepted that too much education rendered a woman unfit for childbearing; rigorous thinking shrivelled the uterus. But as Maria Edgeworth (1767–1849) in *Letters to Literary Ladies* contends, one cannot expect women to have achieved greatness in the arts when they have been denied the resources, i.e., equal access to education: "You demand the work, and deny the necessary materials."[15] Depriving women of an education effectively denies them access to the production of literature. Moulsworth even suggests provocatively that with "necessary materials" women will do more than just rival men's artistic production: with an education women "would in witt, and tongs surpasse / All art of men thatt is or euer was" (ll. 35–36). But the challenge will not be met, for as Moulsworth recognizes, the opportunity is absent not only for her but even more so for other women.

In addition to a lack of education, aspiring women writers would have faced not just indifference, as would be the case for many male writers, but actual hostility. As Woolf remarked, "there was an enormous body of masculine opinion to the effect that nothing could be expected of women intellectually" (*A Room* 56). A belittling or patronizing attitude existed toward women writers, a belief expressed in words Robert Southey addressed to Charlotte Brontë: "Literature is not the business of a woman's life, and cannot be."[16] Criticizing the belief that creativity is a "male quality," Sandra M. Gilbert and Susan Gubar, in *The Madwoman in the Attic*, raise the question, "Is the pen a metaphorical penis?" (3). They write that in "patriarchal Western culture, ... the text's author is a father ... whose pen is an instrument of generative power like his penis" (6). Western culture ascribes a masculine quality to textual production, to creativity: men create, women are created, Pygmalion-like. Moulsworth works against that tenet in her poem and in her assertion of identity. By stating, "My Name was Martha" (l. 17), she significantly supplies only her given name, which alone does not change. The act of naming, like writing, is an act of creation. Moulsworth literally associates her birthday with the birth of the poem: "This season fitly willinglie combines / the birth day of my selfe, & of theis lynes" (ll. 5–6), lines that link creation of self with writing. She creates herself metaphorically and her text literally. Ironically the month is November, a time associated with oncoming winter and death, but for Moulsworth it symbolizes a new beginning. On the one hand, she is fifty-five and in the November of her life, but on the other, she is experiencing a rebirth. In taking pen in hand, Moulsworth asserted herself and undercut the patriarchal theory of creation, in which the metaphorical penis creates and in which women are objects to be created or acted upon.

Women are also silenced because of the demands of the traditional gender roles of wife and mother, roles which Moulsworth accepted. She defines herself through her relationships to a patriarchal God, her father, and her husbands, making no mention of her mother or of any contemporary woman. Women, expected to provide affectionate care, are left with little leisure and solitude, both requirements for writing and both often resulting from financial independence. Significantly enough, Moulsworth wrote her "Memorandum" only when these requirements were met. Recognizing the danger inherent in accepting the commonly ascribed roles for women, Woolf, in her essay "Professions for Women," writes that

> the Angel in the House ... was intensely sympathetic. She was immensely charming. She was utterly unselfish.... She sacrificed herself daily.... she never had a mind or a wish of her own, but preferred to sympathize with the minds and wishes of others.... Had I not killed her she would have killed me. She would have plucked the heart out of my writing.[17]

The sympathy proffered by the "angel" is manifest in Mouls-worth's poem in her portrayals of her father and her husbands. But since they are absent, the "angel" no longer needs to be killed in order for Moulsworth to have the opportunity to write.

Among more recent writers, Adrienne Rich also recognizes from personal experience the dangers of the traditional roles. In *On Lies, Secrets, and Silence*, she writes about the frustration of being a writer and a mother and a wife, eventually being unable to work because of the "female fatigue of suppressed anger and loss of contact with my own being ... partly from the discontinuity of female life with its attention to small chores, errands, work that others constantly undo."[18] She writes about being forced as a woman to choose between societal expectations and "imagination" (45) and between "love" and the "egotism" which led to "creation, achievement, and ambition" (46), choices that men did not have to make. Many women writers (including Willa Cather, Edith Wharton, Katherine Anne Porter, and Eudora Welty) have remained childless; others (like Elizabeth Barrett Browning) had children only after a career was established; and others (like Tillie Olsen) set writing aside until the children were raised. Moulsworth in the 1600's would have been bound by tradition and culture. It is conceivable that her "Memorandum," her only known piece of writing and perhaps her only attempt, was written and could only have been written because the demands of husband and children were no more. At fifty-five she (like many women her age) no longer had a prescribed function in society and was thus free to write her own narrative.

Because of women's position in a patriarchal culture, the autonomy needed to be a writer is often denied women, who (as Tillie Olsen writes in *Silences*) were "Beaten, raped. Bartered. Bought and sold.... Excluded, excluded, excluded from council, ritual, activity, learning, language."[19] Women, as she points out, were "denied one's body. Powerlessness.... Soft attractive graces; the mirror to magnify man. Marriage as property arrangement. The vice of slaves: dissembling, flattering, manipulating, appeasing" (27). Therefore, she concludes, women have lacked a primary attribute of being a writer: the "conviction as to the importance of what one has to say; one's right to say it" (27). Olsen's argument need not be taken literally for it to be relevant, nor was it intended only on a literal level. Women, even if not raped, fear rape, or if not beaten they fear physical violence and often seek protection or limit their activities, both of which in turn diminish their independence and autonomy. While Moulsworth's social position was privileged, her position as a woman in her society was still subordinate: she was "excluded from ... learning, language." In addition, the "vice of slaves" was not unknown to her. Moulsworth writes that she learned Latin, but lest that be threatening, she soon mentions that she has forgotten it. She praises her husbands ("all louely, lovinge all, some more, some lesse" [l. 47]), but when faced with the possibility of a fourth marriage, she chooses a single life. This was a viable option probably because of some financial independence and the reduction of cultural pressure resulting from her age.

Moulsworth's "Memorandum" is clearly deserving of study by feminist critics. But can the poem itself be labelled as feminist? Addressing the question "When is women's art feminist art?", Michèle Barrett points out that "an emphasis on women is not a sufficient condition to make cultural production feminist [but] it must be at least a *necessary* condition.[20] All women's art is not feminist, but all feminist art "could be seen as a category *within* a tradition of woman's art" (Barrett 163). Moulsworth's "Memorandum" is part of a tradition of woman's art. But can it also be categorized as feminist? Definitions of feminist art are often vague. Rosalind Coward considers feminist works those that are overtly linked to feminist political aims or that "chart ... the experience of women's oppression."[21] Cheri Register suggests that feminist literature must advance the political and social goals of attaining equality and promoting a sense of community among women.[22] Moulsworth's poem is the story of one Renaissance woman's life and thus contributes to understanding the totality of female experience: it is one tile in the (as yet incomplete) mosaic. Moulsworth presents a portrait of a self-actualized woman who chooses when she marries, accepts and appreciates her sexuality, manages her household competently, decides not to remarry, and creates a poem in which she advocates equal education of the sexes. She had the ability to achieve a strong sense of identity in spite of a rather restrictive sixteenth- and seventeenth-century culture. Thus the subject and theme of the "Memorandum" can conceivably be seen as feminist, but can the same be said about its structure and language?

Moulsworth's "Memorandum" is a well-crafted poem, adhering to the then-current aesthetic standards—standards set, however, by the patriarchal literary establishment which some feminist critics find suspect. Aesthetic rankings are culturally specific, historically specific, and, therefore, also gender specific. It can thus be argued that Moulsworth is producing what Hélène Cixous terms "Man's writing": "Most women ... do someone else's writing ... and in their innocence sustain it and give it voice, and end up producing writing that's in effect masculine."[23] Moulsworth's poem does succeed according to accepted standards of quality, but since those standards are male, has she violated herself? One might respond by saying that even though there is conformity, her unique female voice is still present. There is an implied questioning and, therefore, an undermining of the patriarchy. Paradoxically, even though she is adhering to established aesthetic standards, simultaneously she is also challenging the patriarchy. Women were believed to be incapable of creative work equal to that produced by men. Moulsworth, in adopting male standards, belies those assumptions. Her voice, added to the voices of all those who preceded and succeeded her, contributes to the crumbling of the patriarchy. As Cixous points out, "logocentrism and phallocentrism ... the conceptual foundation of an ancient culture is in the process of being undermined by millions of a species of mole ... never before known."[24] In other words, women, seemingly insignificant, will "crumble ... the rock upon which they [men] founded this church ... the masculine structure that passed itself off as eternal-natural" (Cixous, *Newly Born* 65). While the damage each woman does is perhaps miniscule, the cumulative effect undermines the entire system.

Moulsworth's poem also poses another question: is written language genderless or are there distinct sexual differences or markings?[25] If differences exist, can they be linked to the sex of the writer and not to another factor, such as class or status? Cheris Kramer, Barrie Thorne, and Nancy Henley contend that in language, "differences of power and status are more salient than those of gender alone."[26] They argue that since women function as a subgroup or muted group in a patriarchal culture, it is their subordination rather than their gender that affects and controls their relationship to language—a relationship which is different than that experienced by the dominant group.[27] Thus perhaps marginality, rather than gender, is the prime cause of differences in language.

Discussions about language, on one level, concern surface features such as sexism and stylistic preferences, but on another level the discussion centers on what language is—a question intimately related to the development of the psyche. French theorists (including Hélène Cixous, Luce Irigaray, and Julia Kristeva) address the issue at this level, searching for a language that is appropriate for or is innate to women, an *écriture féminine* that does not violate women. The discussion of language engaged in by French feminist critics is perhaps not obviously relevant to an analysis of a seventeenth-century poem but is seemingly more relevant to modern and contemporary writers: indeed, the works of Virginia Woolf, Dorothy Richardson, James Joyce, Jean Genet, Marguerite Duras, and Clarice Lispector are often proffered as examples of *écriture féminine*. However, some of the concepts can be beneficial to a reading of Moulsworth's "Memorandum."

Briefly, the works of the French critics are based on ideas of Jacques Lacan, who was himself heavily influenced by Freud. Lacan in *Ecrits* argues that when a child moves from the pre-Oedipal stage into the symblic, he or she acquires language.[28] Since males and females have different experiences in the phallic or Oedipal stage of development, they also have a different relationship to language.[29]

Since the symbolic stage reinforces the patriarchy, women, according to Kristeva, must reject or work against this discourse and draw from the semiotic, the language that is centered in the pre-Oedipal stage—the stage in which the emphasis is on the body, on the maternal connection, and on natural rhythms and not on hierarchy and organization.[30] Likewise, Hélène Cixous, in "The Laugh of the Medusa" and elsewhere, also clearly links *écriture féminine* to the body ("Write your self. Your body must be heard."); to *jouissance* (desire or ecstasy or pleasure); and to a style that disrupts the text with breaks, blanks, and silences.[31] But she avoids defining *écriture féminine* because to do so would in itself be limiting. Irigaray argues that because Western patriarchal discourse relegates women to the position of the "other,"[32] it can only represent women as inferior, as deviating from the standard. Unlike Cixous and Kristeva, she calls for an *écriture féminine* which can only be written by women. She agrees with

Cixous and Kristeva that such writing is not hierarchal or oppositional but "other"; for Irigaray, woman's language "is continuous, compressible, dilatable, viscous, conductible, diffusable" (111). She continues that

> it is useless, then, to trap women in the exact definition of what they mean, to make them repeat (themselves) so that they will be clear; they are already elsewhere ... and if you ask them insistently what they are thinking about, they can only reply: nothing. Everything.[33]

Accepting Irigaray's ideas on language creates a dilemma, for it means accepting something very close to the stereotypical views on women and their use of language that have been set forth by the patriarchal culture, views that suggest that women are illogical, unorganized, and irrational. In fact, as Cixous recognized, defining *écriture féminine* itself poses a problem, since the act of defining leads inadvertently into employing a male standard as a basis for that definition.

Such discussions about *écriture féminine* may represent somewhat utopian ideas about language because women, as Toril Moi notes, "cannot pretend to be writing in some pure feminist realm outside patriarchy" (140). And, she continues, "There is no *other space* from which we can speak: if we are able to speak at all, it will have to be within the framework of symbolic language" (170). But in the blanks, gaps, and silences of patriarchal language, the feminine can be revealed. As Terry Eagleton writes, "It is in the significant *silences* of a text, in its gaps and absences that the presence of ideology can be most positively felt.... the significance of the work lies in the difference rather than unity of the work."[34] Thus the blanks and gaps of texts by women need to be identified and studied. While Moulsworth's use of language clearly falls within practices established by the patriarchal culture, there are gaps or blanks within her logic that lead to an implied questioning of that culture. For instance, rather than being named, she names herself, assuming the subject position. In addition, although she writes that she has forgotten her Latin, it is obvious that her education (as the poem attests) has been valuable. Moreover, although she defines herself through her relationships with men, she more immediately constructs herself through her own narration.

Moulsworth—using male forms, structure, and language to tell her story—is ostensibly doing "man's writing," but the gaps or the silences of her poem imply a feminist message. Even though she defines herself as a daughter, wife, mother, and widow (positions determined by her relationship to men), the poem and, indeed, the act of writing suggest her strength and autonomy. Moulsworth can be included in the list described by Gilbert and Gubar:

> Women from Jane Austen and Mary Shelley to Emily Bronte and Emily Dickinson produced literary works that are in some sense palimpsestic, works whose surface designs conceal or obscure deeper, less accessible (and less socially acceptable) levels of meaning. Thus these authors managed the difficult task of achieving true female literary authority by simultaneously conforming to and subverting patriarchal literary standards. (73)

What Moulsworth has done is to take pen in hand at a time when creativity was seen as a male quality and to narrate her own story, creating herself rather than merely being created, constructing herself as carefully as she constructed her text. In the patriarchal culture she has created her own space, and it is "siluar" (l. 110) and of value.

For as Moi asks, "How could we ever discover the nature of the ideology that surrounds us if it were entirely consistent, without the slightest contradiction, gap or fissure that might allow us to perceive it in the first place?" (124). Moulsworth highlights a crack in the patriarchal ideology of the seventeenth century—a crack that permits an examination of that culture. By her example she demonstrates that women are competent and autonomous when they are supposed to be dependent and subordinate, and that they are intelligent, educated, and creative when they are supposed to be none of these. While on one level she accepts cultural dictates, on other levels she contradicts them. But that contradiction, part of the strength of her text, exposes the flaws of the social order and of the cultural assumptions and at the same time renders the poem an important feminist text.

Notes

1. Annette Kolodny defines pluralism as meaning "that we entertain the possibility that different readings, even of the same text, may be differently useful, even illuminating, within different contexts of inquiry. It means, in effect, that we enter a dialectical process of examining, testing," and, she continues, "our task is to initiate nothing less than a playful pluralism, responsive to the multiple critical schools and methods." See "Dancing through the Minefield: Some Observations on the Theory, Practice, and Politics of a Feminist Literary Criticism," *The New Feminist Criticism: Essays on Women, Literature, and Theory*, ed. Elaine Showalter (New York: Pantheon Books, 1985), 144–67, esp. 160–61.

2. For a comparison of Anglo-American feminist critics with their counterparts in France, see Toril Moi's *Sexual/Textual Politics: Feminist Literary Theory* (London: Routledge, 1985). Moi suggests that since the French criticism is grounded more firmly in theory, it is more rigorous and, therefore, more useful for the study of literature.

3. French critics reserve the word *female* to refer to biological characteristics and *feminine* for attributes based on gender or those that are culturally determined. However, in discussions concerning a tradition of literature by women, Anglo-Americans use *female*, and since this book addresses a predominantly Anglo-American concern, I have adopted their terminology.

4 . Woolf, *A Room of One's Own* (1929; New York: Harcourt Brace Jovanovich, 1957), 68–69.

5. See Showalter, *A Literature of Their Own: British Women Novelists from Brontë to Lessing* (Princeton: Princeton University Press, 1977), 11–12.

6. See Walker, *In Search of Our Mothers' Gardens* (New York: Harcourt Brace Jovanovich, 1983), 14.

7. See Moers, *Literary Women: The Great Writers* (Garden City, NY: Doubleday, 1976).

8. See Edward Wagenknecht, *Nathaniel Hawthorne: Man and Writer* (New York: Oxford University Press, 1961), 150.

9. See Dickinson, *The Poems of Emily Dickinson*, ed. Thomas H. Johnson (Cambridge, MA: Harvard University Press, 1955) and also Browning, *The Complete Works of Mrs. E.B. Browning*, ed. Charlotte Porter and Helen Clarke (New York: Fred DeFau and Company, 1900). In particular, see Dickinson's "Her 'last Poems'—" (# 312) and Browning's "To George Sand: A Recognition."

10. See *The Letters of Elizabeth Barrett Browning*, ed. Frederick G. Kenyon, 2 vols. (New York: MacMillan, 1899), 1: 230–32.

11. See Forrester, "What Women's Eyes See," in *New French Feminisms*, ed. Elaine Marks and Isabelle de Courtivron (New York: Schocken Books, 1980), 181.

12. See Walker, *In Search of Our Mothers' Gardens*, 234.

13. See Pope, "Essay on Criticism," in *Alexander Pope: Selected Poetry and Prose*, ed. Wiliam K. Wimsatt, Jr. (New York: Holt, Rinehart, and Winston, 1965), 63–84. The quoted lines are 139–40.

14. By the same reasoning, novels developing in the eighteenth century were thought to represent a more accessible genre for women because the genre lacked roots in the classical forms and resembled in structure the letters, journals, and diaries that women had already been writing. See Ian Watt's *The Rise of the Novel: Studies in Defoe, Richardson, and Fielding* (Berkeley: University of California Press, 1957) and Ellen Moers's *Literary Women*. See also Juliet Mitchell's *Women: The Longest Revolution* (New York: Pantheon Books, 1982). Mitchell, speculating on why women were drawn to the novel, suggests that the novel was an attempt by women to describe themselves in a period of flux, the change to a capitalistic society.

15. See Edgeworth, "Letters to Literary Ladies," in *The Norton Anthology of Literature by Women: The Tradition in English*, ed. Sandra M. Gilbert and Susan Gubar (New York: W.W. Norton, 1985), 191–94.

16. See Sandra M. Gilbert and Susan Gubar, *The Madwoman in the Attic: The Woman Writer and the Nineteenth Century Imagination* (New Haven: Yale University Press, 1979), 8.

17. See Woolf, "Professions for Women," in *The Death of the Moth and Other Essays* (New York: Harcourt Brace Jovanovich,

1957), 235–48, esp. 236–38. The term "Angel in the House" is taken from the title of a poem by Coventry Patmore (1823–1896).

18. See Rich, *On Lies, Secrets, and Silence: Selected Prose, 1966–1978* (New York: Norton, 1979), 43.

19. See Olsen, *Silences* (New York: Delacorte Press, 1978), 26.

20. See Barrett, "Feminism and the Definition of Cultural Politics," in *Feminist Literary Theory*, ed. Mary Eagleton (Oxford: Basil Blackwell, 1986), 160–63. For the first quote, see 160; for the second, see 163.

21. See Coward, "'This Novel Changes Lives': Are Women's Novels Feminist Novels? A Response to Rebecca O'Rourke's Article 'Summer Reading,'" in *Feminist Literary Theory*, ed. Mary Eagleton (Oxford: Basil Blackwell, 1986), 155–60, esp. 156.

22. See Register, "American Feminist Literary Criticism: A Bibliographical Introduction," in *Feminist Literary Criticism: Explorations in Theory*, ed. Josephine Donovan (Lexington: University Press of Kentucky, 1975), 1–28, esp. 19.

23. See Cixous, "Castration or Decapitation," *Signs* 1 (1976): 41–55, esp. 52.

24. See Cixous and Catherine Clement, *The Newly Born Woman*, trans. Betsy Wing (Minneapolis: University of Minnesota Press, 1986), 65.

25. In speech, distinct differences have been found in language use: women insert more qualifiers or hedges, add tag questions, and employ a questioning intonation when none is required. See Robin Lakoff's *Language and Women's Place* (New York: Harper and Row, 1975) and Dale Spender's *Man Made Language* (London: Pandora, 1980).

26. See Cheris Kramer, Barrie Thorne, and Nancy Henley, "Perspectives on Language and Communication," *Signs* 3 (1978): 638–51, esp. 641.

27. Victor A. Thompson, in his study of organizational behavior, identified speech patterns between superiors and subordinates that are similar to those found between men and women. See his book *Modern Organization* (New York: Alfred A. Knopf, 1961).

28. See Lacan, *Ecrits: A Selection* (New York: W.W. Norton, 1977).

29. For a discussion of Lacan's position, see Jane Gallop's *The Daughter's Seduction: Feminism and Psychoanalysis* (Ithaca, NY: Cornell University Press, 1982) and her *Reading Lacan* (Ithaca, NY: Cornell University Press, 1985). See also Luce Irigaray's *This Sex Which Is Not One*, trans. Catherine Porter (Ithaca, NY: Cornell University Press, 1985).

30. See Julia Kristeva, *Desire in Language: A Semiotic Approach to Literature and Art* (New York: Columbia University Press, 1980).

31. See Cixous, "The Laugh of the Medusa," *Signs* 1 (1976): 875–93, esp. 880.

32. As early as 1952, Simone de Beauvoir had examined the relegation of women to the position of the "other" in all areas of the culture; see her book *The Second Sex* (New York: Vintage Books, 1974).

33. Ann Rosalind Jones presents a critique of the French theories of language; see her article "Writing the Body: Toward an Understanding of *l'écriture féminine*," in *The New Feminist Criticism: Essays on Women, Literature, Theory*, ed. Elaine Showalter (New York: Pantheon Books, 1985), 361–77. Jones points out that a woman's concept of her body is culturally determined and, therefore, tainted by the patriarchal culture. Jones also suggests that a child's introduction to language is much more closely related to the mother than to the father.

34. See Eagleton, *Marxism and Literary Criticism* (Berkeley: University of California Press, 1976), 34–35.

BIBLIOGRAPHY

Barrett, Michèle. "Feminism and the Definition of Cultural Politics." In *Feminist Literary Theory*, edited by Mary Eagleton, 160–63. Oxford: Basil Blackwell, 1986.

Beauvoir, Simone de. *The Second Sex*. 1959. New York: Vintage Books, 1974.

Beilin, Elaine V. *Redeeming Eve: Women Writers of the English Renaissance*. Princeton: Princeton University Press, 1987.

Benstock, Shari. "Authorizing the Autobiographical." In *The Private Self: Theory and Practice of Women's Autobiographical Writings*, edited by Shari Benstock, 10–33. Chapel Hill: University of North Carolina Press, 1988.

————. *The Private Self: Theory and Practice of Women's Autobiographical Writings*. Chapel Hill and London: University of North Carolina Press, 1988.

Bottrall, Margaret. *Every Man a Phoenix: Studies in Seventeenth-Century Autobiography*. London: John Murray, 1958.

Boxer, Marilyn J., and Jean H. Quataert, eds., *Connecting the Spheres: Women in the Western World, 1500 to the Present*. New York and Oxford: Oxford University Press, 1987.

Brodzki, Bella, and Celeste Schenck, eds. *Life/Lines: Theorizing Women's Autobiography*. Ithaca and London: Cornell University Press, 1988.

Browning, Elizabeth Barrett. *The Complete Works of Mrs. E.B. Browning*. Edited by Charlotte Porter and Helen Clarke. New York: Fred DeFau and Company, 1900.

————. *The Letters of Elizabeth Barrett Browning*. Edited by Frederick G. Kenyon. 2 vols. New York: MacMillan, 1899.

Bruss, Elizabeth W. *Autobiographical Acts: The Changing Situation of a Literary Genre*. Baltimore and London: The Johns Hopkins University Press, 1976.

Cerasano, S.P., and Marion Wynne-Davies, eds. *Gloriana's Face: Women, Public and Private, in the English Renaissance*. Detroit: Wayne State University Press, 1992.

Cixous, Hélène. "Castration or Decapitation." *Signs* 1 (1976): 41–55.

————. "The Laugh of the Medusa." *Signs* 1 (1976): 875–93.

————, and Catherine Clement. *The Newly Born Woman*. Trans. Betsy Wing. Minneapolis: University of Minnesota Press, 1986.

Coward, Barry. *The Stuart Age: A History of England, 1603–1714*. London and New York: Longman, 1980.

Coward, Rosalind. "'This Novel Changes Lives': Are Women's Novels Feminist Novels? A Response to Rebecca O'Rourke's Article 'Summer Reading.'" In *Feminist Literary Theory*, edited by Mary Eagleton, 155–60. Oxford: Basil Blackwell, 1986.

Crawford, Patricia. "Women's Published Writings: 1600–1700." In *Women in English Society: 1500–1800*, edited by Mary Prior, 211–82. London and New York: Methuen, 1983.

Cross, F.L., ed. *The Oxford Dictionary of the Christian Church*. London: Oxford University Press, 1966.

Delaney, Paul. *British Autobiography in the Seventeenth Century*. New York: Columbia University Press, 1969.

Dickinson, Emily. *The Poems of Emily Dickinson*. Edited by Thomas H. Johnson. Cambridge, MA: Harvard University Press, 1955.

Eagleton, Terry. *Marxism and Literary Criticism*. Berkeley: University of California Press, 1976.

Edgeworth, Maria. "Letters to Literary Ladies." In *The Norton Anthology of Literature by Women: The Tradition in English*, edited by Sandra M. Gilbert and Susan Gubar, 191–94. New York: W.W. Norton, 1985.

Ferguson, George. *Signs and Symbols in Christian Art*. New York: Oxford University Press, 1954.

Ferguson, Margaret W., Maureen Quilligan, and Nancy J. Vickers, eds. *Rewriting the Renaissance: The Discourses of Sexual Difference in Early Modern Europe*. Chicago and London: University of Chicago Press, 1986.

Ferguson, Moira, ed. *First Feminists: British Women Writers, 1578–1799*. Bloomington: Indiana University Press, 1988.

Forrester, Viviane. "What Women's Eyes See." In *New French Feminisms*, edited by Elaine Marks and Isabelle de Courtivron, 181–82. New York: Shocken Books, 1980.

Friedman, Susan Stanford. "Women's Autobiographical Selves: Theory and Practice." In *The Private Self: Theory and Practice in Women's Autobiographical Writings*, edited by Shari Benstock, 34–62. Chapel Hill and London: University of North Carolina Press, 1988.

Fuller, Thomas. *Church History of Great Britain*. Edited by J.S. Brewer. 6 vols. Oxford: Oxford University Press, 1845.

Gallop, Jane. *The Daughter's Seduction: Feminism and Psychoanalysis*. Ithaca, NY: Cornell University Press, 1982.

———. *Reading Lacan*. Ithaca, NY: Cornell University Press, 1985.

George, Margaret. *Women in the First Capitalist Society: Experiences in Seventeenth-Century England*. Urbana and Chicago: University of Illinois Press, 1988.

Gilbert, Sandra M., and Susan Gubar. *The Madwoman in the Attic: The Woman Writer and the Nineteenth Century Imagination*. New Haven: Yale University Press, 1979.

Goreau, Angeline. *The Whole Duty of a Woman: Female Writers in Seventeenth Century England*. Garden City, NY: Doubleday, 1985.

Graham, Elspeth, Hilary Hinds, Elaine Hobby, and Helen Wilcox, eds. *Her Own Life: Autobiographical Writings by Seventeenth-Century Englishwomen*. London and New York: Routledge, 1989.

Great Britain. Historical Manuscripts Commission. *Calendar of the Manuscripts of the ... Marquess of Salisbury*, part XV. London: HMSO, 1930.

Greer, Germaine, Susan Hastings, Jeslyn Medoff, and Melinda Sansone, eds. *Kissing the Rod: An Anthology of Seventeenth-Century Women's Verse*. New York: Farrar Straus Giroux, 1989.

Gunn, Janet Varner. *Autobiography: Toward a Poetics of Experience*. Philadelphia: University of Pennsylvania Press, 1982.

Haselkorn, Ann, and Betty S. Travitsky, eds. *The Renaissance Englishwoman in Print: Counterbalancing the Canon*. Amherst: University of Massachusetts Press, 1990.

Henderson, Katherine Usher, and Barbara F. McManus, eds. *Half Humankind: Contexts and Texts of the Controversy about Women in England, 1540–1640*. Urbana and Chicago: University of Illinois Press, 1985.

Houlbrooke, Ralph A. *The English Family: 1450–1700*. London and New York: Longman, 1984.

Houston, R.A. *Literacy in Early Modern Europe: Culture and Education, 1500–1800*. London and New York: Longman, 1988.

Irigaray, Luce. *This Sex Which Is Not One*. Trans. Catherine Porter. Ithaca, NY: Cornell University Press, 1985.

Jankowski, Theodora A. *Women in Power in Early Modern Drama*. Urbana and Chicago: University of Illinois Press, 1992.

Jardine, Lisa. *Still Harping on Daughters: Women and Drama in the Age of Shakespeare*. Totowa, NJ: Barnes and Noble, 1983.

Jones, Ann Rosalind. "Writing the Body: Toward an Understanding of *l'écriture féminine*." In *The New Feminist Criticism: Essays on Women, Literature, Theory*, edited by Elaine Showalter, 361–77. New York: Pantheon Books, 1985.

Kadar, Marlene. "Coming to Terms: Life Writing—from Genre to Critical Practice." In *Essays on Life Writing: From Genre to Critical Practice*, edited by Marlene Kadar, 3–20. Toronto: University of Toronto Press, 1992.

Kanner, Barbara, ed. *The Women of England from Anglo-Saxon Times to the Present: Interpretive Bibliographical Essays.* Hamden, CT: Archon Books, 1979.

King, Margaret L. *Women of the Renaissance.* Chicago and London: University of Chicago Press, 1991.

Klein, Joan Larson, ed. *Daughters, Wives, and Widows: Writings by Men about Women and Marriage in England, 1500–1640.* Urbana and Chicago: University of Illinois Press, 1992.

Kolodny, Annette. "Dancing through the Minefield: Some Observations on the Theory, Practice and Politics of a Feminist Literary Criticism." In *The New Feminist Criticism: Essays on Women, Literature, and Theory,* edited by Elaine Showalter, 144–67. New York: Pantheon Books, 1985.

Kramer, Cheris, Barrie Thorne, and Nancy Henley. "Perspectives on Language and Communication." *Signs* 3 (1978): 638–51.

Kristeva, Julia. *Desire in Language: A Semiotic Approach to Literature and Art.* New York: Columbia University Press, 1980.

Lacan, Jacques. *Ecrits: A Selection.* New York: W.W. Norton, 1977.

Lakoff, Robin. *Language and Women's Place.* New York: Harper and Row, 1975.

Masek, Rosemary. "Women in an Age of Transition: 1485–1714." In *The Women of England from Anglo-Saxon Times to the Present: Interpretive Bibliographical Essays,* edited by Barbara Kanner, 138–82. Hamden, CT: Archon Books, 1979.

Mason, Mary G. "The Other Voice: Autobiographies of Women Writers." In *Life/Lines: Theorizing Women's Autobiography,* edited by Bella Brodzki and Celeste Schenck. Ithaca and London: Cornell University Press, 1988. 19–44.

Mendelson, Sara Heller. "Stuart Women's Diaries and Occasional Memoirs." In *Women in English Society 1500–1800,* edited by Mary Prior, 181–210. London and New York: Methuen, 1985.

Metford, J.C.J. *Dictionary of Christian Lore and Legend.* New York: Thames and Hudson, 1983.

Mitchell, Juliet. *Women: The Longest Revolution.* New York: Pantheon Books, 1982.

Moers, Ellen. *Literary Women: The Great Writers*. Garden City, NY: Doubleday, 1976.

Moi, Toril. *Sexual/Textual Politics: Feminist Literary Theory*. London: Routledge, 1985.

Neuman, Shirley. "Autobiography: From Different Poetics to a Poetics of Differences." In *Essays on Life Writing: From Genre to Critical Practice*, edited by Marlene Kadar, 213–30. Toronto: University of Toronto Press, 1992.

Nussbaum, Felicity A. "Eighteenth-Century Women's Autobiographical Commonplaces." In *The Private Self: Theory and Practice of Women's Autobiographical Writings*, edited by Shari Benstock, 147–71. Chapel Hill and London: University of North Carolina Press, 1988.

Olney, James. *Metaphors of Self: The Meaning of Autobiography*. Princeton: Princeton University Press, 1972.

Olsen, Tillie. *Silences*. New York: Delacorte Press, 1978.

Osborn, James M. *The Beginnings of Autobiography in England*. Los Angeles: William Andrews Clark Memorial Library, 1959.

Otten, Charlotte F., ed. *English Women's Voices, 1540–1700*. Miami: Florida International University Press, 1992.

Pope, Alexander. "Essay on Criticism." In *Alexander Pope: Selected Poetry and Prose*, edited by William K. Wimsatt, Jr., 63–84. New York: Holt, Rinehart, and Winston, 1965.

Prior, Mary, ed. *Women in English Society 1500–1800*. London and New York: Methuen, 1985.

Register, Cheri. "American Feminist Literary Criticism: A Bibliographical Introduction." In *Feminist Literary Criticism: Explorations in Theory*, edited by Josephine Donovan, 1–28. Lexington: University Press of Kentucky, 1975.

Rich, Adrienne. *On Lies, Secrets, and Silence: Selected Prose, 1966–1978*. New York: Norton, 1979.

Rose, Mary Beth. "Gender, Genre, and History: Seventeenth-Century English Women and the Art of Autobiography." In *Women in the Middle Ages and the Renaissance: Literary and Historical Perspectives*, edited by Mary Beth Rose, 245–78. Syracuse: Syracuse University Press, 1986.

Rowlands, Marie B. "Recusant Women: 1560–1640." In *Women in English Society 1500–1800*, edited by Mary Prior, 149–80. London and New York: Methuen, 1985.

Schenck, Celeste. "All of a Piece: Women's Poetry and Autobiography." In *Life/Lines: Theorizing Women's Autobiography*, edited by Bella Brodski and Celeste Schenck, 281–305. Ithaca and London: Cornell University Press, 1988.

Showalter, Elaine. *A Literature of Their Own: British Women Novelists from Brontë to Lessing*. Princeton: Princeton University Press, 1977.

Smith, Hilda L. *Reason's Disciples: Seventeenth-Century English Feminists*. Urbana, Chicago, London: University of Illinois Press, 1982.

Smith, Sidonie. *A Poetics of Women's Autobiography: Marginality and the Fictions of Self-Representation*. Bloomington and Indianapolis: Indiana University Press, 1987.

———, and Julia Watson, eds. *De/colonizing the Subject: The Politics of Gender in Women's Autobiography*. Minneapolis: University of Minnesota Press, 1992.

Spender, Dale. *Man Made Language*. London: Pandora, 1980.

Spengemann, William C. *The Forms of Autobiography: Episodes in the History of a Literary Genre*. New Haven and London: Yale University Press, 1980.

Springer, Marlene, ed. *What Manner of Woman: Essays on English and American Life and Literature*. New York: New York University Press, 1977.

Stone, Lawrence. *The Family, Sex and Marriage in England: 1500–1800*. Abridged ed. New York: Harper & Row, 1979.

Thompson, Victor A. *Modern Organization*. New York: Alfred A. Knopf, 1961.

Tilley, Morris Palmer. *A Dictionary of the Proverbs in England in the Sixteenth and Seventeenth Centuries*. Ann Arbor: University of Michigan Press, 1950.

Todd, Barbara J. "The Remarrying Widow: A Stereotype Reconsidered." In *Women in English Society: 1500–1800*, edited by Mary Prior, 54–92. London and New York: Methuen, 1985.

Travitsky, Betty. "'His Wife's Prayers and Meditations': MS Egerton 607." In *The Renaissance Englishwoman in Print: Counterbalancing the Canon*, edited by Anne M. Haselkorn and Betty S. Travitsky, 241–62. Amherst: University of Massachusetts Press, 1990.

———. "Introduction: Placing Women in the English Renaissance." In *The Renaissance Englishwoman in Print: Counterbalancing the Canon*, edited by Anne M. Haselkorn and Betty S. Travitsky, 3–41. Amherst: University of Massachusetts Press, 1990.

———, ed. *The Paradise of Women: Writings by Englishwomen of the Renaissance*. New York: Columbia University Press, 1989.

Wagenknecht, Edward. *Nathaniel Hawthorne: Man and Writer*. New York: Oxford University Press, 1961.

Walker, Alice. *In Search of Our Mothers' Gardens*. New York: Harcourt Brace Jovanovich, 1983.

Warnicke, Retha M. *Women of the English Renaissance and Reformation*. Westport, CT: Greenwood Press, 1983.

Watt, Ian. *The Rise of the Novel: Studies in Defoe, Richardson, and Fielding*. Berkeley: University of California Press, 1957.

Wilcox, Helen. "Private Writing and Public Function: Autobiographical Texts by Renaissance Englishwomen." In *Gloriana's Face: Women, Public and Private, in the English Renaissance*, edited by S.P. Cerasano and Marion Wynne-Davies, 47–62. Detroit: Wayne State University Press, 1992.

Wilson, Katharina M., ed. *Women Writers of the Renaissance and Reformation*. Athens and London: University of Georgia Press, 1987.

Woodbridge, Linda. *Women and the English Renaissance: Literature and the Nature of Womankind, 1540–1620*. Urbana and Chicago: University of Illinois Press, 1984.

Woolf, Virginia. "Professions for Women." *The Death of the Moth and Other Essays*. New York: Harcourt Brace Jovanovich, 1957.

———. *A Room of One's Own*. 1929. New York: Harcourt Brace Jovanovich, 1957.

Wrightson, Keith. *English Society: 1580–1680*. New Brunswick, NJ: Rutgers University Press, 1982.